JAPAN IN THE PASSING LANE

JAPAN IN THE PASSING LANE

An Insider's
Account
of Life
in a Japanese
Auto Factory

SATOSHI KAMATA

Translated and edited by Tatsuru Akimoto

■ ■ ■   ■ □ ■   ■ ■ ■

Introduction by Ronald Dore

PANTHEON BOOKS, New York

Library of Congress Cataloging in Publication Data
Kamata, Satoshi, 1938–
    Japan in the passing lane.
    1. Automobile industry workers—Japan.
2. Seasonal labor—Japan.   3. Toyota Jidōsha Kōgyō
Kabushiki Kaisha.   4. Kamata, Satoshi, 1938–
I. Dore, Ronald Philip.   II. Title.
HD8039.A82J3413   1983   331.7′6292′0924 [B]
ISBN 0–394–52718–6   82–47881
                              AACR2

Manufactured in the United States of America

First American Edition

Design by Robert Bull

CONTENTS

v

Translator's Note

Satoshi Kamata, the author of numerous books, is one of Japan's leading free-lance journalists. Much of his writing deals with Japanese industry and labor.

The impetus for *Japan in the Passing Lane*, Kamata's third book, came in large part from conversations with a friend who had been a seasonal worker for several years at Honda manufacturing plants. He told Kamata of the grim working conditions—the boredom, monotony, and incessant work demands—and of the high turnover rate of both regular workers and lower-management employees. Kamata wanted to experience the situation firsthand and chose Toyota because he had heard that the working conditions there were much harsher than at other automobile plants in Japan. Kamata stayed at Toyota for the full term of his six-month contract, and the diary he kept there forms the basis of this book.

Kamata was married, and while he worked at Toyota his wife and two small children lived at home a few hundred miles away. Kamata's experience of loneliness and extended separation closely parallels that of many farmers in Japan who do seasonal work at various plants and construction sites away from their families during their slack periods on the farm.

There are two points that could be raised about the book: it was written some time ago, and it deals primarily with seasonal workers. To these points, Kamata answers as follows:

> This book depicts the realities of 1972–73. If the situation has changed at all, it is only in the sense that the work has become much more difficult, the levels of production greatly increased, and the workers' frustrations more widespread than ever. The only real difference is that the work situation is worse and the competitive power of Toyota stronger.
>
> The numbers of seasonal workers have been reduced in the time since I worked at Toyota, and *oen* (reinforcement workers from other shops) as well as robots have been taking the place of seasonal workers. But the nature and problems of assembly-line work are unchanged for both seasonal and regular workers. Robots have been introduced only in jobs requiring painting, welding, and the like. A robot that can work on the assembly line has yet to be invented.

While *Japan in the Passing Lane* is a sobering examination of Japanese management techniques, Satoshi Kamata's personal concerns are larger:

> I wanted to show the inhumanity of it all—not only its inhumanity but also the unquestioning adherence to such a system. Is the prosperity of a modern, industrial society worth such a cost, such a cruel compulsion of robotlike work? If the production of cars —mere machines—necessitates such a sacrifice of human freedom, just what does this say about the paradox of modern civilization?

Satoshi Kamata's story becomes more important with each passing day.

TATSURU AKIMOTO
July 1982

Introduction

Since long before Chaplin depicted it all in *Modern Times* the large factory assembly line, particularly the automobile assembly line, has been a symbol of the very particular form of degradation which an advanced, relatively affluent, mechanized society imposes on some of its members. There are numerous studies of such work from the outside, but rather fewer articulate subjective accounts by those who have actually lived the assembly-line life as ordinary workers —or at least as workers not privileged by more than their own ability to stand apart, reflect, and write as well as simply work. The reader of English can find a number of American accounts, and at least one translation each from France, from Sweden, and from Hungary.* But from Japan, while Robert Cole's excellent *Japanese Blue Collar*† gives fascinating perspectives on a medium-sized firm, a young American

---

* Studs Terkel, *Working* (New York: Pantheon Books, 1974); Robert Linhart, *The Assembly Line*, trans. Margaret Crosland (Amherst: University of Massachusetts Press, 1981); Göran Palm, *The Flight from Work*, trans. P. Smith (Cambridge: Cambridge University Press, 1977); Miklos Haraszti, *A Worker in a Worker's State*, trans. Michael Wright (New York: Universe Books, 1978).

† Robert E. Cole, *Japanese Blue Collar: The Changing Tradition* (Berkeley: University of California Press, 1971).

in a Japanese engineering shop can hardly pass, or be treated, as an ordinary worker. So we must be grateful to Satoshi Kamata, and to his translator, for giving us this first slice of Japanese assembly-line life available in English. And we must be grateful, too, that when he decided to use his journalist talent on factory reportage he made a beeline to the heart of what by all accounts is one of Japan's most beehive-like enterprises, the Toyota Motor Company.

Kamata's account is direct and unadorned, and by that token convincing. Within the genre, his is one of the closest to being something like the account of "an ordinary worker." It is subjective, to be sure; we hear a great deal about the physical exhaustion he feels and his reactions to his surroundings, but he does not turn analysis of his emotions into an occasion for developing literary conceits in the way more self-absorbed writers do. We do not find him talking, for instance, in the manner of the French writer Linhart, about "the wretched square of resistance against the empty eternity of the work station," nor do we find him attributing his own reactions to other workers, as one suspects Linhart is doing when he discerns in the dreamy, motionless faces of Algerians sitting in front of their Sunday afternoon beers "the anxiety about passing time . . . the painful awareness of each wasted minute which brings them nearer to the roar of the assembly line." The interpretative reflections interspersed with Kamata's direct descriptions—as when he looks around the canteen at his fellow workers and remarks that the few who stand out as having some individuality of gesture or expression are nearly always temporary workers—are more firmly rooted in observation and evidence.

What he does share with Linhart, and with Haraszti writing from Hungary, is a complete and resentful rejection of the whole system. He does not take the broader perspective of a Palm, who can describe the asperities and indignities of factory work but still be thinking realistically about alternatives—accepting that, on the whole, society at large benefits from having cars and typewriters made as efficiently and hence as cheaply as capitalist firms are making them, but asking if it cannot be done, albeit a little less efficiently, in a way that does not require such a sacrifice of dignity and individuality.

That kind of sober Swedish reasonableness is not the style of the Japanese left, which still sees the primary task as being to evoke moral condemnation of the system as it exists. And Kamata's indictment is a powerful one. It is not so much the physical demands of the work which impress. We sympathize with the torments of Kamata's first month, when he is still in the process of acquiring the fluency of movement needed to assemble his gear boxes in his alloted one minute and fourteen seconds, in a constant state of physical exhaustion. But by the end of his time he can clearly cope. The sacrosanct production targets are primarily met, not by speed-up of the line so much as by constant extension of the periods of overtime— which is made more acceptable by the fact that, if it adds to the exhaustion, it adds to the pay packets as well.

And loss of overtime is imposed as a punishment for a young worker who smuggles a girl into his dormitory room! It is that which is more likely to stir the American or British reader—stirred this reader, at any rate—the tight surveillance, the claustrophobic requirement of conformity in word, deed, and thought. No doubt it does powerfully disturb the repose of shift-working bachelors to hear a girl's giggles from the other side of a none-too-soundproof dormitory wall, but that a worker's freedom to lead his own life needs to be set against that seems to occur to no one. The dormitory supervisor observes comings and goings, enters rooms without a by-your-leave, and, Kamata believes as a matter of course, opens letters. Privacy is not a value Toyota seeks to maximize: even a man's biorhythms and what time he goes to bed are a matter of the firm's concern if they are likely to have any bearing on his productive efficiency or his proneness to accidents.

It is all like nothing so much as an army camp. And joining Toyota as a regular worker is indeed rather more like joining the army in America than like going to work for General Motors. You can expect to get "posted" from one plant to another and even have to uproot the family as a consequence. You can expect to have your leave canceled in an emergency; Kamata's foreman is telephoned and called in to cover unexpected absences on a day he had planned to take off. A worker killed in an accident can, if he has been a good worker, expect a posthumous promotion: a new cap with an extra stripe around the rim will adorn his coffin. And the break-time conversation that Kamata records resembles nothing so much as the grumbling of wartime soldiers, full of seemingly alienated complaints about authority turned always, as he notes, to end in the joke which is the indication of acceptance, of the fact that one has made all the choices one can make and there is nothing to do but "soldier on."

In the case of Toyota this is a little more than an

analogy, as Kamata makes clear. The firm has very close connections with the Self-Defense Forces and makes a strenuous effort to recruit former soldiers and NCOs; 2,500 of its workers and a tenth of its foremen are ex-soldiers. It is primarily a matter of ideological affinity, no doubt, though Kamata notes Toyota's interest in sizable orders for defense equipment. More recently, with gloomy forecasts for the long-term future of car markets, Toyota is widely thought to be casting longing eyes at the possibilities for tanks.

The security guards are some of the least attractive characters among Kamata's dramatis personae and seem, indeed, to behave very much like the military police of the system. In part their behavior seems mere officiousness, as when they reprove Kamata for smoking. But when he goes back as a reporter with a camera, it is clear that there is more to it than that. Prying and critical eyes are not wanted—least of all by the complaisant union, which is always ready to cooperate with the guards to defend the company's good name against its enemies.

That defensiveness betrays an awareness that Toyota is open to criticism. It is an indication that by the contemporary standards of Japanese society the extent to which Toyota is so *single-mindedly* devoted to success and the extent to which it suppresses individuality and privacy in a quasi-military organization to achieve it are, as the Japanese would say, *sukoshi ōba* —somewhat overdoing it. That is why it would be wrong to take Kamata's account as entirely typical of work in modern Japan. Many firms *are* like that, and some smaller ones, especially those which, like Toyota, are also outside the main metropolitan centers, are probably worse. But most allow the individual to breathe a little more freely, and most big firms have not managed, or tried, to beat their union into quite such submissive complaisancy as Toyota has.

My own experience of Toyota may not be representative—in half a day one does not sample very much of a firm of Toyota's size—but it did confirm the impression of a more conformist and regimented company than most I have visited in Japan. My business was to inquire about energy conservation measures, and I spent a couple of hours being genuinely impressed by plant engineers who described the ingenious ways they had found to reduce unnecessary pressure in process air systems, cut down heat loss in the foundries, and so on. Having been equally impressed in a steelworks a couple of days before when I happened by chance on a "show and tell" meeting of quality circles and heard a shop-floor worker describe with great competence how his team had thought up a way of revamping the sea-water cooling system they operated in order to save energy, I asked about the contribution of quality circles and workers' suggestions in Toyota to the business of energy conservation. By the end of lunch it had been arranged for me to hear a special presentation by one of the subforemen who had recently won a commendation at his department's "show and tell" session. It was rather different from the matter-of-fact, workmanlike account I had heard at the steelworks, and distinctly less impressive. It might be worthwhile to give some extracts from my notes on the occasion.

M. was a team chief and leader of a group of nine workers, one of fifty-four into which the 370 employees of the power department were divided. He had been leading the group for five years and told his story with the help of an overhead projector and sixty transparencies, many of them in cartoon form.

The group was known as the Hottomanzu (Hot Man's) Group. Its basic spirit was to emphasize harmony and cooperation. The four pillars of the house of improvement were cooperation, initiative, harmony, and work satisfaction. They held meetings twice a month, but things did not go very well in the initial period, which he called the "groping in disorderly darkness period." A lot did not come to the meetings. There was a tendency for a few to monopolize the discussion. Too much depended on the leader. Too many had the attitude: Tell me what to do and I'll do it. Let those who are keen be keen if they want; other people can do what they like; I'm getting on with my own job.

M. decided that some stimulus was needed. He proposed that they should set themselves the objective of winning a prize for group achievements. There was opposition on the grounds that it was too difficult to be effective because it was not a production department. M. convinced them that even in the boiler house improvements were possible. They actually did get a prize for a project to improve the efficiency of an electric furnace. But there were still too many reluctant passengers, people who thought they were just being too obedient to orders from above. Here M. decided that new methods were necessary. He got engineers to come to advise on particular technical problems. At one stage he declared a three-month moratorium on meetings so that they could start again with fresh enthusiasm. He rated the contributions of his group members under various headings: speaking, reporting back, doing the summary work for reporting, cooperativeness, attendance, contribution to solving problems, etc. He studied the personalities of the members of his group to see how they could be better integrated into a harmonious team, and introduced the habit of shouting "good morning" the first thing on entering the shop in a firm, loud, positive, and enthusiastic voice until even the misanthropes were forced to respond.

And so it went on. Later he started meetings at 7:30 A.M. instead of after work (in the workers' own time, though from 1980 onward the firm began to offer overtime pay for two or three hours of meetings a month). They taught themselves the various quality-analysis techniques of Pareto diagrams, histograms, graphs, critical path analysis, etc., but being employed in maintenance of a system that was not much capable of alteration, their net achievements over the years seem to have been improved methods of testing the relays which cut out unnecessary motors and a new drill for releasing people trapped in lifts, which involved relocating the tools in the engine housing room, and painting footprints and instructions on the floor to show who should stand where to do what when.

One other caveat against reading Kamata's account as typical of contemporary Japan: he was writing about the last year of the pre-oil-crisis growth period when the shortage of labor was at its height. Wages had been rising quite fast, and this did make a firm's competitive success depend more on getting the maximum production out of each hour of paid labor time. Hence the speed-up which Kamata's friend A. reports as having transformed Toyota's assembly lines from relatively casual and leisurely places some five years before. But rising labor costs were not the most important thing because, although real wages rose fast, productivity per worker was rising slightly faster—by 2.1 times for manufacturing as a whole between 1965 and 1973, when real wages just about doubled. The more important constraint for a firm like Toyota was to get enough workers at all (short of bidding up wages to a degree that would damage their competitive position). Hence the resort to high levels of overtime, and hence the drive to recruit more temporary workers. Overtime of thirty-five to forty hours a month was then very common throughout Japanese manufacturing. When the recession came in 1975 it dropped sharply: statistics for average overtime hours fell by 50 percent.

The flexible ability to change production hours without increasing overhead labor costs is, of course, the attraction to the firm of using overtime to meet an increase in demand. And seasonal workers who are employed on short contracts of three to six months serve the same purpose of maintaining flexibility. Their numbers in manufacturing were also sharply reduced in the 1975 recession, but in 1972 they were very much in demand, and at a premium. The advertisement which brought Kamata to the factory advertised for both seasonal workers and ordinary workers. The seasonal workers were to get $250 a month basic pay and up to $300 with overtime. The ordinary workers, who could acquire tenure after a probationary period, had an age scale ranging from $207 at age twenty to $282 at thirty-five (calculated, the advertisement says, on the assumption of twenty-five hours of overtime a month), though their bonuses would be considerably greater than the "thank-you bonus" of four-and-a-half days' wages which Kamata received at the end of his six months. The picture common in the West, of Japanese manufacturing as divided into a labor aristocracy of unionized elite workers in the large firms and a much larger substratum of workers in small workshops, on-site subcontractors, and temporary workers in the same large firms, was true of the 1950s. Then it was only the bright pupils in each school-leaving class of fifteen-year-olds who could expect to pass on to a "good" job with tenure, seniority payments, and the like. The rest had to content themselves with one of the other jobs without the security *and* with lower pay levels. A labor shortage in the 1960s, and the fact that tenured jobs were widely available to anyone who could stand the irksomeness of them, meant that temporary workers' wages had to be raised to include an implicit compensation for the lack of security, thus considerably altering the picture of a segmented labor economy with a privileged minority and a deprived majority.

In 1972, then, the high levels of overtime and the strong demand for seasonal workers which Kamata describes at Toyota were typical of Japanese firms. With the recovery since 1975, the overall statistics for manufacturing show overtime as coming back, if not quite to 1972 to 1973 levels. But temporary workers are less in evidence. How the situation currently is in the motor industry at large, or at Toyota in particular, I had hoped to be able to tell the reader, and I wrote to the Toyota personnel office for statistics. Unfortunately I had no reply, though a middle manager did fly to see me from Brussels to express his surprise that a respected scholar, author of X, Y, and Z (his research had been thorough), should be concerning himself with such a scurrilous work by an embittered nobody. I thought he might be going to offer a thank-you bonus for the sincere interest I was showing in Toyota's affairs, but instead he left promising to expedite a reply from the personnel office—though warning me that they are always very busy . . .

One of the things which gives depth to Kamata's account, and one which convinces us of its integrity, is the fact that, for all his alienation, he still admits, for instance, to feeling guilty about leaving the line early, and he does not conceal the fact that by the end of his six months he had become a model worker, under strong pressure from his superiors to stay. It is not surprising, given the atmosphere. The contrast with Linhart's Citroën factory is sharp. A French radical going into a French factory finds a place where discipline is tough and antagonisms not far below the surface; where the line sometimes gets turned on only by the iron hand of the stopwatch-wielding supervisor over the howling protests of the workers who think they have been cheated of thirty seconds of their ten-minute break. In such an atmosphere it is not difficult for the working-observing intellectual to keep his alienation on the boil. (I use the word here, of course, in its colloquial sense of alienation from the firm—harboring a resentful antagonism against it—not as a subtly obscure piece of sociological jargon.) But it is clear that Toyota is not like that; it is harder for Kamata to keep his sense of antagonism sharp because his fellow workers are not alienated. Their grumbling is real enough, and they are initially angry enough about, for instance, the apparently unilateral decision to work an extra Saturday shift. But even about that, they are resigned to the likelihood that the union will agree with the company that the shift is necessary, and hardly see themselves as victims of injustice. Their grumblings are a railing against their fate, but a fate which is seen as dictated by the necessity of the company's competitive struggle with Nissan, not by the heartlessness of managers or the greed of the owners of capital. Hence the way their grumbles turn into "soldiering on" jokes. And hence it is possible, as Kamata tells us incidentally, for the company to send one of his workmates back to his former regiment to try to recruit some of his friends in full confidence that he will tell a good story of the advantages of working for Toyota.

It is the more difficult for Kamata to retain a sense of spiritual distance because his fellow workers are so friendly. They help each other out when they are behind with their work, and rarely exchange an angry word. Kamata records not a single instance of harsh bitterness, not a single muttered obscenity. The lavatory graffiti are mild enough for a girls' convent school. These are gentle people, as one realizes when he describes the friendly dormitory neighbor who drops in to introduce himself and goes back to bring his ashtray in order not to mess up the room, or the young men who spend their wages on stuffed animals to put beside their pillows.

And this is not the camaraderie of the oppressed, of men seeking refuge in fellowship from the harshness of superiors; it is a camaraderie which *includes* the foreman and team leaders. Kamata records how his initial clumsiness evokes some impatience from the foreman in his first days, but not harsh words of blame. A worker who tries to catch up by sorting parts during the break is told by the foreman that he ought to get his proper rest. The oppression the workers feel—and undoubtedly they do feel it—is not the oppression of coercive external authority. It comes from inner compulsion bred from submission to the norms and targets which the organization has set for them. "The foreman was absent, so we had to work harder to make up for him" is one of the book's most revealing phrases.

The social and authority distance between workers and foreman is much less than between foreman and section manager—as is apparent early on in the book when new output targets are handed down and we hear, I think, the book's only expression of recalcitrant protest to superior authority. The distance from worker to section manager is even greater. That workers do sometimes harbor stronger antagonisms toward these more remote bosses is clear from Kamata's account, but even there it does not take a great deal to win loyalty. The section manager who goes on lecturing the shop about safety so long that they miss their noodles and then, when he realizes it, is so stricken by remorse that he buys everybody buns and ice cream out of his own pocket thereby wins at least one worker's devotion for life.

Model worker or not, that much acceptance of authority Kamata never achieves. He still has quite enough distancing reactions to confide to his diary. One fascinating incident where his responses are sharply opposed to those of the other workers is the accident to a team chief who loses the top joint of his third finger. When the general foreman calls everyone together for a safety talk, it is not to tell people that you can get hurt if you're not careful but that careless-ness leading to accidents shows inconsiderateness to-ward everyone else. It appears that the safety system penalizes everybody when an accident happens; the section becomes a "designated safety campaign shop" with arm bands and slogans and inspections and meetings in the lunch break. The foreman and managers have their bonuses reduced, and it puts the section manager one strike down for his promotion record. Kamata's reaction is: the accident was caused by the excessive work pressure and inadequate safety protection on the machines. If the firm really cared about safety it would do something about those things instead of all this exhortation. His friends' reactions are: nobody is to blame, really. For all the safety precautions on the machines, accidents are bound to happen, and it's reasonable to have these consciousness-raising schemes for reducing them. What bad luck for the section manager who was just about to get the shop out of "designated safety-campaign shop" status when this had to happen.

Which is the more sensible judgment? It is difficult for an outsider to say. Japan has got its present affluence, Kamata's fellow workers have their cars, his friend Takeda can enjoy his weekend mountaineering trips, Kamata can get home across half Japan to see his pregnant wife (and he can find a market for his books), because, over a century of forced-pace, catching-up industrialization, efficiency and greater output have been made priority goals and the capitalists and managers and foremen who make decisions in these matters were prepared to subordinate the safety of human lives to those goals. One thing one can be certain of is that the trade-off involves a far smaller cost in limbs and lives now than it did in the appalling conditions that prevailed—in the mines especially—at the beginning of the century. In fact, if one takes simply deaths from industrial accidents as posing the fewest problems for international comparison, the 1973 figures (the latest I have to hand, but there is no reason to think it an exceptional year) show that in manufacturing Japan had the same three deaths per 100,000 workers as the United States— slightly lower than Britain's four. (In mining Japan was a shade higher than the other two countries; in construction, equal with Britain and higher than the United States; in the railroads, much lower than either.) Things are undoubtedly safer now in Japanese factories than they have ever been, but some, like our author, still think that they are not safe enough. And who is to say that he is not right? There are other voices, too, being raised in Japan to urge that Japan is affluent enough now to start changing the terms of the trade-off a little faster, to sacrifice output a little more readily not only for safety but for more leisure, more personal freedom, and perhaps even—though it is surprising how little it is talked of in spite of the eloquent testimony of people like Satoshi Kamata—a more relaxed pace of work.

If the book might carry that message for Japanese readers in its Japanese context, its translation will have an equally interesting but different significance for its American and British readers. Kamata, of course, was writing a profoundly political book for quite clear political motives. The translation is also likely to be greeted with clearly political enthusiasms—if from partisan positions of which Kamata was hardly aware when he wrote.

He certainly did not foresee that ten years later the Japanese motor industry would be desperately trying to fend off the protectionist attacks of its American and European competitors, or that his American publishers would want to change the title (he had called it *Automobile Factory of Despair*) to *Japan in the Passing Lane*. The venom displayed by the UAW local which performed a ritual destruction of a Toyota car will certainly inspire strident quotations of Kamata's book as offering proof that Japanese workers are grossly exploited and that it is unfair competition, not inefficiency, which is robbing the United States domestic industry of its markets.

They would be wrong, of course. The uncomplaining diligence of the Japanese workers may be a part of it; in spite of a further 20 percent rise in real wages between 1972 and 1979, Japanese firms probably still have to pay less wages per unit of effective effort than American firms, though certainly not less than British firms. But the big difference in efficiency—what brought the number of man-hours required per vehicle down by 1979 to some 53 percent of the 1970 figure—is the enormous volume of capital investment in new equipment in Japan and the devoted ingenuity with which Japanese engineers have learned to get the most out of it. Where heavy manhandling jobs and tedious repetitive jobs of the kind Kamata describes still remain, they are doubtless performed at much the same intensity as ten years ago, but a lot of these jobs have by now been automated or robotized out of existence—and often with improved quality controls built into the process as well. Those are the sources of Japanese competitiveness to which Americans and Europeans would do well to pay attention.

But there is another, much more interesting, debate in the context of which Mr. Kamata will almost certainly, and very relevantly, be quoted. The "learn from Japan" movement is at its height. *The Art of Japanese Management** has become a best-seller; the quality circle is offered as a magic recipe for instant transformation of a factory's productivity record. Already the Ford union has accepted a Japanese-style deal which embodies Japanese-type lifetime employment guarantees and a cooperative attitude to productivity improvements.

There are many in labor union circles—more explicitly and emphatically in Britain than in America—who are deeply suspicious of such moves as a subtle capitalist plot to "incorporate" and "co-opt" workers into the system, to substitute docility for militancy and so make the world safer for capitalist exploitation. So you see—those who have these reactions will doubtless say when they read Kamata's account—*this* is what it's all about. Quality circles may sound harmless enough, but go down *that* road and here's where you end up: a lot of emasculated, work-crazed automatons imprisoned in a system which robs them of any control over their own lives.

It is entirely true that the sort of cooperative attitudes implicit in the quality-circle idea—the idea I mentioned earlier as being impressively exemplified by the steelworker group with its revamped cooling system, that everybody in the plant should have the chance to take part in improving the product and the process, and that given the opportunity most people

---

* Richard T. Pascale and Anthony G. Althos, *The Art of Japanese Management* (New York: Simon & Schuster, 1981).

could and would want to take part—is at variance with the attitudes traditional in Anglo-Saxon, particularly British, industry.

The difference is not only that the Japanese-type cooperative approach rejects the zero-sum view of worker-capitalist relations—the idea that everything that benefits the one side must represent an equal and balancing loss to the other. Most unions, even in Britain, have moved beyond that stage and agree in principle that cooperation between management and unions can bring benefits to both sides. But what is lacking in Britain is trust in the mechanisms which determine how the benefits achieved by cooperation will be distributed. Hence the determination of trade unions in Britain, where they have traditionally exercised control over the work situation (that is, over the effort side of the wage-effort bargain) to make sure the bargain over who gets the benefits is signed and sealed *before* the cooperation takes place: "We will agree to work the new machine which will save the company X pounds a year, if and only if we get our fair share of that in a wage increase of Y pounds a week."

What the quality-circle idea requires is sufficient *trust* in the fairness of the overall distribution of the proceeds—between workers' wages and managers' salaries and shareholders' dividends—to feel sure that the extra benefits of individual efforts to improve productivity will also be fairly shared. Once that trust is there, workers may well find that looking for ways of doing the job better can make their lives rather more interesting—even if the improvements sometimes complicate the lives of others, as Kamata found when an oil line appeared above his work station one day and an extra task was added to his assignment.

Toyota workers apparently have that trust. The 200,000 improvement suggestions a year, which Kamata contrasts with the miserable 20 grievances processed through the union machinery, doubtless include a vast number tortuously produced from empty heads by workers anxious only to fulfill their "suggestion norms," or some desperate ploy by men such as the foreman whose rhetoric I experienced to prove their leadership by notching up achievements for their groups. But they also include, doubtless, a number of genuinely bright ideas which gave a lot of satisfaction to the workers who thought them up, as well as a real increment of efficiency to the company. (The best ideas are usually rewarded with prizes, generally of not much more than token size, and generally consumed in drinks at a work-group party.)

Toyota workers "belong to" their firm; British and American workers "work for" their firm—have an employment contract with it (X hours a week performance of Y job function for Z pounds or dollars). The various institutional devices of the employment system in Japan which contribute to creating this difference are well known: the employment security, the implicit contract of a job until retirement age; the union structure based on the enterprise, not on the occupation or the industry or political affiliation; the company-based welfare services and training schemes; and above all the wage system based, not on job functions in a short-run contract, but on seniority and skill scales which look for fairness over the working lifetime (a system such as European civil services have always had and as I G Metall, the leading German union, is proposing should be adopted in Germany as the best way of handling technological change in industry).

There are management consultants who peddle the idea of quality circles as if it were something like computer-aided design that a manager can decide to "put into" the existing structure of his capitalist firm, leaving the rest of the employment system untouched. This is clearly fraudulent. A worker's willingness to offer his ideas and extra efforts to promote the company's success depends in part on a sense of belonging to the firm, on the ability of the firm to mobilize what one might call "membership motivation" as opposed to "market motivation" ("I do what I'm paid to do; no less, but no more"). And the features of the employment system listed above—the institutional acceptance by the firm that all its workers as well as its shareholders have claims on it—are an essential part of the context which permits that sense of belonging to be fostered.

Those institutional features can be transferred; a lot of what count as progressive firms in Britain and America have some of them already. And there is good reason to believe, if one looks at the British civil service, or the armies and police forces of the two countries which have such employment systems, that they could work to promote a sense of belonging-ness there, too. But would they also, in their Japanese form, promote the second ingredient which evokes those 200,000 suggestions from Toyota workers: the sense of trust in the decisions of superiors, the acceptance of the way the system acts to distribute rewards as being basically fair? Or is there something else, something which has to do with national character, in the way Kamata's colleagues accept the authority of their superiors? Does their trust rest on attitudes to authority which are common in Japan but rare in other, at least in English-speaking, countries? Or, perhaps, does their cooperativeness rest, not on trust in the fairness of the system at all, but on resigned submissiveness?

There is a lot of circumstantial evidence that the answer is yes. I mean the evidence from all sorts of social situations of the extent to which subordinates overtly defer to the authority—and to the status right to receive deference—of their superiors. Pupils are not only more deferential to teachers than elsewhere (a few cases of adolescent dropouts showing mild violence against their teachers have aroused intense alarm about the onset of anarchy); they are also deferential to older pupils. If you travel a commuter train in late afternoon when the children are going home, and younger pupils get off at an earlier stop than their seniors, you will hear them shout out in the sort of ritual yell with which sergeant majors report to their officers that the company is all present and correct: "Excuse us for getting off first." The way junior civil servants or managers carry the briefcases of their seniors as a matter of course; the way department stores employ little girls to bow, doll-like, at the foot of every moving staircase and say in bell-clear automaton tones: "Thank you for patronizing our store" (and the fact that the average customer is presumably pleased, not revolted and embarrassed, by this show of deference): all these features, soon obvious to the most casual visitor to Japan, betoken attitudes which make it understandable that Kamata's friends should have taken the production targets they were given as not to be challenged, that they should have grumbled furiously about some of the decisions of higher management or of the union hierarchy, but not seriously thought that their authority could be challenged.

The difference between that and the world of a British or American worker is not primarily, if at all, that the one is being conned and the other is more aware of his own interests; it is not even a matter of false consciousness and true class consciousness. It is as much as anything, I suspect, a difference in the implications of personal subordination for self-respect. Trollope describes Mr. Bunce, one of the few trade unionists in his nineteenth-century world, as always longing "to be doing some battle against his superiors, and to be putting himself in opposition to his employers—not that he objected personally to Messrs Foolscap, Margin and Vellum, who always made much of him as a useful man;—but because some such antagonism would be manly, and the fighting of some battle would be the right thing to do." Not by any means the whole truth about nineteenth-century British trade unionism, but an important part of it. If Southern European machismo is about sex and fighting between equals, Northern European machismo centers around the hidden injuries of authority relations. Kamata clearly has a little of the same spirit, and that is what makes him something of a deviant in his factory setting.

But let us not forget that the cultural differences between Japan and Britain are not limited to differences in the attitudes of subordinates. The ways bosses exercise, and believe they ought to exercise, authority are correspondingly different. Doubtless Mr. Bunce's Margin, Foolscap, and Vellum, however they "made much of" Mr. Bunce, believed that the way to handle men was by firmness and strength of personality; fairness, yes, but firmness above all; make the men respect you, preferably with a respect that contains a little more fear than affection; an unwavering steely eye is the greatest asset a handler of men can have; a "master" should keep himself aloof, avoiding any vulgar chumminess, which will only lead to "the men" taking liberties; give them an inch and they will take an ell, etc., etc.

Japanese men generally dislike being at such emotional arms-length from each other, even from—or especially from—their subordinates. Hence all the systems such as Kamata notes for treating sections as work *groups*, including managers and workers, which share a collective responsibility when an accident happens in the section and have to bear collective sanctions which weigh more heavily on those in superior positions. Hence the caring *style* of authority, of the foreman who spends a lot of his time helping out the slower workers. Superiors in Japan are expected to have the Confucian virtue of benevolence. And their need to make good their claim to be responsible guardians of the welfare of everybody in the firm does act as a restraint on the extent to which they can claim for themselves the lion's share of the benefits. The spread of wage-salary differentials is narrower within the typical Japanese firm than in the typical American firm. In almost any firm a skilled worker with twenty-five years' seniority will be getting more than any twenty-five-year-old graduate manager.

Benevolence is an efficient way of running a factory, provided—and it is an important proviso for understanding the difference between, say, Britain and Japan

—managers also have the virtue of competence. One of the factors which predisposes Japanese workers to accept the authority of their managers is the fact that Japan is a more throughgoing meritocracy than any except the Eastern European industrial countries. In the bureaucratized Japanese corporation the managerial ranks are open only to men with a university degree (with rare exceptions, such as the one Kamata records, of promotions to lower managerial rank of very senior workers); the difference between a manager and subordinate workers is perceived as being, not a difference between a privileged scion of the middle class set in authority over workers born and bred of the working class, but a difference between those who were sufficiently good at school to make it into a university and those who were not. It is left to a few educational sociologists to point out that class background as well as ability does have powerful effects in deciding who gets to the university; the general public—and even the opposition political parties—are content to accept that the system is fair and that those who have the degrees that set them on managerial ladders deserve them. Japan's educational system is a quite powerful factor in legitimating the hierarchy of authority in the Japanese corporation.

One of the reasons why the class factors in educational success are not a matter of great debate in Japan is because the cultural differences between the middle and working class—differences in accent, bearing, leisure tastes, style of family life—are far less than in a country like England or France, and less even than in the United States. The similarity between managers and workers extends to their attitudes to work. Managers expect to work just as hard as manual workers;

they feel no particular need to defend their superior status by demonstrating that they can afford a leisurely pace, or by wearing a smart suit and keeping their hands clean.

The further one goes into these complexities of authority relationships in the various national manifestations of the hierarchical bureaucratic organization—that ancient invention which has only in the twentieth century come to dominate all our lives—the harder it becomes to give sensible answers to either of the two related questions which Kamata's account raises about the "learn from Japan" movement: on the one hand the manager's question, "Could I work a Japanese system and have only a few disgruntled Kamatas to deal with?" and on the other hand the labor leader's question, "Does Kamata tell us all we want to know? Start with quality circles and they'll make work-crazed zombies out of us all before they've finished."

Let me try to give my answer to the manager's question first. By all means try your quality circles. Try basing the employment relation on the assumption that workers *can* develop membership motivation as well as market motivation and are willing to take initiatives to make the firm they belong to a success. You will find, in the first place, that the employment system has got to be such—has got to give guarantees of security and thoughtful treatment that are such—that the feeling of belonging really is generated. Secondly, you will find that for the belongingness to be more than resigned there is a need to generate a feeling of trust that the benefits of a firm's success will be fairly distributed. In most areas of the United States and Britain this is not something likely to be spontaneously provided by the cultural milieu as it is in Japan. Some people in both countries certainly do grow up with a predisposition to believe that the people who get to positions of authority are on the whole likely to be benevolent and fair and ought to be deferred to, but, *not* growing up in a culture where first-year students have to bow to second-year students or where the propriety of deference is demonstrated every day by little girls in department stores and obsequious interviewers talking to cabinet ministers on television screens, far fewer do so than in Japan. Low-key, non-self-assertive, hard-working, and caring styles of authority, allied with sheer work competence, may well take you a long way towards building up the necessary trust. The accounts of Japanese-managed firms in England and Wales which have been studied by British researchers suggest this.* But these are mostly in Britain's fringe industrial areas, and perhaps are firms with a selected, or self-selected, work force. Something more is likely to be needed if the essential "trust in fairness" is to be created in the hard core of the older industrial areas where militant, and on past performance justified, suspicion of all bosses is more deeply ingrained.

There, I suspect, a good deal more is necessary: primarily, learning to trust people more and let them *know* more. That means, first of all, letting them know more about the rationale for their work and for their production targets and letting them make suggestions about them. You have to have the faith that the short meetings which Kamata's work group were constantly having can be taken out of working time and still pay off in an improvement in the quality of the work effort

---

* Michael White, "Japanese Management and British Workers," *Policy Studies* 2 (July 1981): 49–58.

in the remainder of the time. Secondly, it means letting workers know how the benefits of the enterprise's collective efforts are distributed—as, at present, neither the capitalist firms of the United States or Britain nor the communist firms of Haraszti's Hungary do let their workers know—much less have a say in—who gets what. Profit-sharing schemes are a possible start; inevitably workers' representatives will want to know how the accounting variable "profit" is calculated, the rationale for making a division between directors' salaries and their bonuses, and so forth. If profit sharing comes with works councils, or more formal patterns of industrial democracy which provide a means for manual workers' representatives to have as much say in the determination of managers' salaries as vice versa, the chances of building up the "trust in fairness" which makes quality circles workable would be much improved. Genuinely democratic corporate forms do not *guarantee* trust—as studies of Yugoslavia show—but they most certainly help, and probably nothing less will suffice.

To the unionist, reading Kamata in the context of a "learn from Japan" attempt to put quality circles in his factory and deeply suspicious of a plot to emasculate the workers, I would say this. If your problem is Mr. Bunce's problem and you cannot easily live with yourself unless you are defying some authority, then it is perfectly sensible of you to oppose any blurring of us/them lines with devices such as quality circles. Similarly, if you are one of that even rarer group of people who really do believe (as opposed to making a militant pose of believing for the satisfaction of Buncite antinomian urges) that one day capitalism will be superseded by socialism if only the working class can hold together and keep its us/them consciousness intact, and if you can also believe that hierarchial bureaucratic organizations will somehow not exist in that socialist state, or will somehow be more benign than the one where Haraszti worked in Hungary, then again you would be justified in digging in your heels and saying: Over my dead body.

But if you accept that with modern technology the nature of industrialism has changed, that there is no way that we can maintain our standard of living without large organizations, and that the technical requirements of the division of labor in such organizations inevitably give them hierarchical patterns of authority, and further, that the efficiency of such organizations (and hence the maintenance and improvement of standards of living) depends on relations of trust and cooperation between the different levels of the hierarchy: if you accept that, then a different strategy might be more sensible. Embrace the quality circles, embrace the assumption that workers can willingly contribute initiatives (and not just routine fulfillment of contract) to improve efficiency in the firm of which they are members. But build on that notion of membership to insist that the assumptions behind quality circles must involve other changes too, changes to make sure that the managers do not use their authority in technical matters (which may be necessary because they are matters requiring a competence which only they have) to arrogate to themselves or their shareholder friends more than a fair share of the proceeds of the firm's efficiency. Insist, that is to say, on creating institutions within the enterprise which will make managers accountable to other members of the enterprise, and enable workers not simply, through collective bargaining, to press for the maximum they think they can get, but to take a full part in discussions about what does constitute fairness in the distribution both of effort and of the resulting benefits among all parties with claims on the enterprise.

In short, if one is looking for a lesson from Japan in a firm like Kamata's Toyota, it is not that the holistic corporation-as-extended-family organization with its spirit of cooperation and sense of purpose and its ability to meet production targets should not be, or cannot be, transplanted to countries like Britain and the United States. The holistic cooperative corporation can be hierarchical in authority, over distributional as well as technical matters as it is in Japan, requiring from its lower-ranking members that trustful submissiveness which Kamata was unwilling—and unusual in being unwilling—to give. But it can also be more democratic in distributional matters, requiring that trust should be based on the accountability of managers to the other members of the firm. And if we are to transplant, the latter is the variety that has the better chance of healthy growth in a society which has a good many more workers with intimations of Buncism than workers like Kamata's friends, whose first reaction to an accident is to feel sorry for the manager who will consequently have blotted his safety record.

The submissiveness requirement, in short, can be separated out from the holistic-corporation recipe. And so can the intense, almost frenetic pace of work, which is, after all—far more than the way the corporation requires submissive conformity—the basis of Kamata's indictment of Toyota.

Let us reflect, for a moment, on what started the

recent "learn from Japan" boom. It was not that knowledgeable Americans looked at Japan and saw there a harmonious and benign society which embodied certain eternal values better than their own. What happened was that the competition of Japanese firms came to threaten the markets of American firms at home and abroad, not just, as hitherto, in products like textiles, but in sophisticated fields of high technology. As Chrysler was followed into crisis by General Motors and by Ford, corporation executives began to get anxious. The title of Ezra Vogel's *Japan as Number One** perfectly encapsulates the mood which set in as the alarm bells rang. To a European the somewhat amusing thing about all the heart-searching which followed Vogel's book is that both sides of the argument—both those who approve of his prescriptions that America should take a leaf from Japan's book and those who remain unshaken in their belief in America—accept as their basic premise that in a perfectly ordered world it is naturally the United States which should be number one, and that if that can be shown not to be the case then the times really are out of joint and something should be done to put them back in joint again. Britain's "learn from Japan" movement has somewhat more modest aims (the search for something that might at least slow down the decline in Britain's competitiveness), is largely derivative, being inspired from the other side of the Atlantic, and is pursued with less conviction. (The *Financial Times* chose for its 1981 April Fool spoof the story of a

---

* Ezra F. Vogel, *Japan as Number One: Lessons for America* (Cambridge, Mass.: Harvard University Press, 1980).

Californian firm which purportedly set out to learn from Japan by the total-package method—not just quality circles and open-plan offices but also raw fish in the canteen and special overcrowded commuting facilities, on the grounds that since one didn't know *what* it was about Japanese methods that made them so efficient, one could only imitate in everything. The reader was being invited to be amused not only at the idea of learning from Japan but at the earnestness of American beliefs that the key to the ultimate is always just around the corner.)

But what if the intense pace of work and the long hours at relatively low (time-and-a-quarter) overtime rates turn out to be the larger element in the total package of Japanese competitiveness, not the superior organizational virtues of Japan's management system or of a system of employment which breeds membership motivation? There are doubtless many corporation executives in America who would still want to take lessons from Japan, and teach Americans the virtues of hard work again. So also in Britain. There doubtless are some naïve ones who actually see devices like quality circles as just another way of squeezing more work out of workers at no increased cost, thereby fully justifying the suspicions of labor unions.

If there are managers with such hopes, they are asking for the moon. The decline of the work ethic with increasing affluence does seem to be a one-way street, and short of catastrophe or dictatorship it seems unlikely that either Britain or America is going to travel any way except the conventional one along it. And Japan is going the same way too. Kamata reported in 1972 the union's proposals for a five-day week (very quaintly put not as a union demand for workers' welfare but as a suggestion about how the firm should respond to the social needs of the age). OECD figures for 1979 still have the average Japanese worker at work for over 2,100 hours a year— 200 more even than Britain, and nearly 400 more than Germany or France. There is still a long way to go before the length of the working year in Japan is reduced to European or American levels, but reduced it almost certainly will be. It is possible that the pace of work during working hours will also relax (though by no means certain; I am far from sure, though these things are difficult to measure, that the work pace in Kamata's shop was in fact greater than in Germany or the United States). At any rate, wage costs per worker-hour are almost certain to rise to a level higher than that of Japan's competitors. Then, and only then, shall we know how much of Japan's present competitiveness was due to the work ethic and how much to organization and the employment system.

Meanwhile, we must be grateful to Satoshi Kamata for making us think of these things afresh, for helping us to respond in a slightly more informed and less naïve manner to "learn from Japan" prescriptions, and for reminding us—even if he does not convince us that international competitiveness is not a good thing to have—of what the human cost of international competitiveness might be.

RONALD DORE
Technical Change Centre, London
May 1982

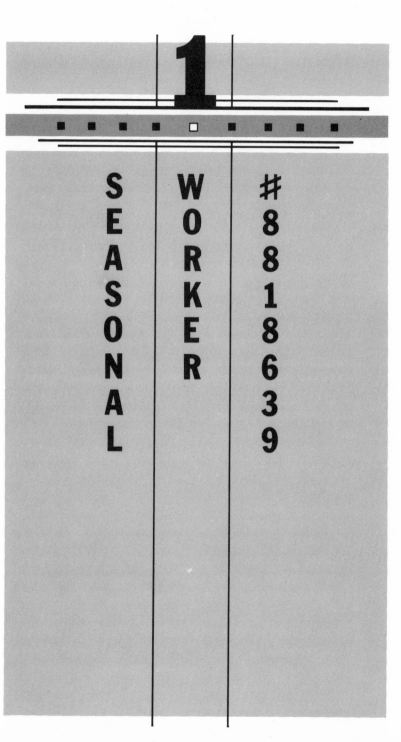

1

SEASONAL WORKER #8818639

Tuesday, September 12, 1972—3:31 P.M.

The super-express train arrives at the Nagoya station on time. The new workers are to rendezvous "in front of the wall painting just outside the ticket gate." The station is crowded with people who are obviously sightseers from the country. As I walked toward the meeting point, I see a Panasonic flag. I walk farther, somewhat distracted by the flag. Suddenly I almost run into a banner with the words "Toyota Motor Company, Ltd." on it. I had planned to approach the meeting place slowly, feeling out the situation, so my first impulse is to walk away. But a short, stout man holding the little blue banner quickly spots me and flashes a smile. I acknowledge him with a bow and ask him, in a northern accent, "Has a man called Kudo, from Hirosaki, already arrived?"

"I don't know, I haven't called the roll yet. The men left their baggage in lockers and are wandering around. Come back at four-thirty, will you?" He speaks easily, as though he has repeated these words often enough. He is alone. I can't see any baggage that might belong to the other seasonal workers, my future comrades. I hadn't quite expected this. Could they really be such carefree travelers? It makes me feel a little strange to know that these seasonal workers fresh from the country are roaming the streets loose and carefree.

I spend an hour reading newspapers in a coffee shop

near the station. When I return, there are already more than a dozen men waiting. Most of them are young, a little over twenty, I'd guess. Jeans, long hair—some of the fellows with it dyed blond. The middle of September is still a busy season for farmers in the field, so these can't be farmers' sons. Most of them must be from other cities, looking for jobs.

My friend Kudo is there, wearing the same white-checkered gray summer jacket he wore at the interviews. The jacket hangs loose on his shoulders. He's looking around uncertainly. I gesture and approach him, but he doesn't recognize me.

For about half an hour until the company bus arrives, the seventeen of us wait in line at the edge of the pavement. We stand silently, smoking, none of us talking. Only three or four in the group are over middle age, obviously heads of families from the country. They are the true "seasonal workers." The rest are young. They carry their belongings in department-store shopping bags. None of them stand out. Any one of them could easily disappear, swallowed up by a typical city crowd.

Finally a big bus with the Toyota logo painted on it arrives. Once inside, we keep silent, even after the bus starts moving. We all feel awkward. We drive through downtown Nagoya and then up and down hills surrounded by rice fields. By now, it's twilight. Inside the bus, the radio news reports that the first snow of the year has fallen on Mount Fuji—"two inches of snow at the summit."

Kudo has two small traveling bags and two over-stuffed department-store shopping bags. An umbrella and a pair of rubber boots stick out of one of the bags. He has been hired as a seasonal worker, but he hopes to become a regular employee in the company. When we were interviewed at the Public Employment Security Office, I was surprised to read what he had put on his personal information card. In the column marked "Motive for Choosing Toyota," he had written "Toyota has bright prospects." For an unknown seasonal worker whose contract would automatically expire after six months, "bright prospects" was a pretty big mouthful. But that one line, without irony or humor, expressed this twenty-year-old man's burning desire to "enter" the world of big enterprise. Our interviewer had terminated the conversation with a vague "We'll see in six months."

The bus drives through gently rolling hills for thirty or forty minutes, though for me it feels more like an hour. I'm beginning to feel depressed.

When big factory buildings and company-owned houses appear, we know we are almost there. Finally, the bus stops in front of a four-story concrete building behind a chain-link fence. It's already dark. On the building is a signboard that says "Sei-shin Wafu Ryo" (Sacred Heart and Pleasant Breeze Dormitory). This seems to be our new home. No building less suits its name; it looks more like a prison camp. There's even a guardhouse with glass windows beside the gate. The dormitory houses students of the Toyota Company Vocational High School, workers sent on loan from the Daihatsu Motor Company, and seasonal workers who are undergoing "preparatory education." We go in and join those who have already arrived. There are forty of us in all—five to a room. We receive meal tickets for supper and breakfast, as well as sheets and pillowcases starched so stiff they crackle. A guard yells at Kudo for smoking a cigarette.

5

After taking baths and eating supper, there's nothing more to do. We settle down in a wide room bare of furniture and soon begin to chat. Besides Kudo and me, there are two other young men: Sato, twenty-two years old, from Fukuoka, and Kajiya, twenty-three, from Fussa, near Tokyo. This is the first time any of us have been seasonal workers for Toyota, but the fifth man—tall and dark, probably over fifty, with an air of self-assurance—has been here twice before.

Sato is a young guy with a square jaw and a dauntless expression on his face. He's short but well built. After graduating from high school, he worked in a steel factory. He has applied to join the Self-Defense Forces,* but has not yet been admitted. His family laughed at him and teased him, saying, "You can't be a good Japanese citizen if you're rejected even by the Self-Defense Forces." He's come to Toyota a little angry and wondering why the Self-Defense Forces don't want him.

Kajiya, a tall guy with long eyelashes, has the air of a city boy, but he has actually been in the Self-Defense Forces in Bihoro, Hokkaido, for two years. Naturally, Sato and Kajiya quickly strike up a lively conversation about guns and other weapons. Sato's knowledge of armaments is amazing. He knows by heart the thickness of different nations' tank armor and the effective range of all sorts of firearms. Kajiya talks about the efficiency of different rifles, some of which he has actually handled. Kudo and I, naïve country people from the north who know nothing about these things,

---

* In Japan the armed forces are called the Self-Defense Forces because the postwar Constitution forbids the existence of armed forces. [Editor's note]

just sit there and marvel at their knowledge. We lie on the straw floor mat with our heads propped up on our elbows and shake our heads.

Wednesday, September 13

Up at seven. By eight, we are riding a bus to the main gate of the Main Plant.* From there, we walk to the Education Building at the rear of the Main Plant. There are more than thirty of us in the group, and though I assume someone is directing us, we get lost on the way. It turns out that we're blindly following those who have been here before. Still, we find the third-floor orientation room before the scheduled 8:30 meeting.

After calling the roll, the instructor directs us to sit in order according to our home towns. Those from the north are to sit in front. The first seat is taken by a guy from Otaru, Hokkaido, who's over forty and has been here once before. I sit next to him. Then comes Kudo. Next to Kudo sits a man who arrived from Aomori in his new Corona Mark II. His wife owns a bar, and he has been an instructor at a driving school. The four of us sit at the same long desk.

Before the medical examination, the instructor asks if we want an advance to buy meal tickets. Kudo and I borrow $23† each. The man from Aomori asks for $33. The maximum is $33, and most of the men ask for it. Then the medical examination starts: height,

---

* "Main Plant" refers to the oldest plant, located at the Head Office.
† All dollar figures appearing in this book have been calculated at 300 yen to the dollar, which was the exchange rate at the time of these events. [Editor's note]

weight, X-ray, eyesight, color-blindness test, urinalysis, grasping power, spinal-column power, and lung capacity. It's not a simple medical exam, rather a series of tests of physical strength. These are the tests that determine which jobs a worker receives in the company.

After the tests we are divided into groups of seven or eight and ordered to strip to our undershirts and stand in single file. We're asked to jump, squat, stand on one leg, stretch and bend our arms, move our fingers, and rotate our ankles. Before us stands a man in white, intently watching. With his legs wide apart, his body leaning slightly forward, he looks for all the world as if he's judging horses and cows. Actually, he's examining us to see if we will function well as manpower. Humiliating!

After we get dressed and are dismissed, we walk with meal tickets in hand to the canteen in front of the main plant. As soon as the noon siren blows, workers in dirty caps and work clothes pour out of the gate. They quickly climb the stairs and form a line, filling the place. Everyone pushes forward, grabbing an aluminum tray, a plastic mug, a pair of chopsticks, a dish of food from the carts where they are piled, and finally, a bowl of rice from the counter. We have to hustle to get a table. As soon as we've finished, we dump the leftovers into a big garbage drum, carry our dishes and bowls to the sink, and pile up our trays. From beginning to end, not a gesture is wasted. Everything is done with machinelike precision. Throughout the entire meal, I don't see one person talking or laughing. The whole scene makes me lose my appetite.

In the afternoon, we fill out forms for health and unemployment insurance. We also fill out an individual card with our employment history and our family history. These cards will be filed in the personnel department. Each card has a blank space for retirement date. Most of the men automatically write down their contract-expiration date (from three to six months, depending on the individual's wish) and are corrected by the guy in charge.

Finally we see a film called "Thirty Years' History of Toyota, Dedicated to You." The opening, with its long line of trucks along a muddy road (in China, it seems) during World War II, is a shocking reminder that Toyota owes much of its expansion to military production. The film shows the "official" history of the Toyota Motor Company up to the present day.

Pictures of the Toyota strike in 1950* appear in the film, but there's no explanation in the narration. How many of these new workers know the true facts of the strike?

---

* In 1950 there was a major labor dispute at Toyota. The company had continually delayed payment of wages owing to a chronic shortage of funds. The union protested, and in the winter of 1949 the management and union reached an agreement whereby, in return for a 10 percent wage cut, the company promised to stop delaying wage payments and not to fire any employees. However, the delays continued, and in April 1950 the union called a twenty-four-hour strike. The company countered with a "general request for voluntary resignation" and another 10 percent wage cut. In Japan, it is customary for a company not to fire people. Instead, employees are "encouraged" in various subtle ways to "voluntarily resign." Over the following two months the workers protested with mass demonstrations, rallies at workshops and company housing, and mock courts to "try" the directors and the plant manager. However, Toyota finally won the dispute, and in the end 2,146 employees were fired.

9

Thursday, September 14

Like yesterday, the orientation starts at 8:30. Today, we learn the most important rules:

Work Regulations:

1. Don't divulge secrets learned during work.
2. Try hard to increase efficiency and productivity.
3. Follow instructions concerning your duties.

Conditions for Discharge:

1. If the employee is no longer needed.
2. If the employee has physical problems.
3. If the employee is absent for more than twenty days because of an accident outside his work.
4. If the employee is absent for more than fifteen days for personal reasons.
5. If the employee is absent for more than four days straight without reporting.

These regulations are given orally. It is also emphasized that anyone who makes serious or intentional mistakes is to assume responsibility and make compensation.

Then, an "Orientation Manual," edited by Toyota's Department of Education, is handed to each one of us. Using this pamphlet as a textbook, the various section leaders carry out the orientation. Concerning safety and accident prevention, the pamphlet reads: "Always remember *arrangement, order, cleanliness,* and *cleaning*. Remember that it is very important to keep your working environment in order."

How can this be enough to prevent accidents? Is it

simply up to the workers to watch out for themselves if they don't want to get injured?

Another manual, "Safety in General Operations," written by the company Safety and Sanitation Office, says:

---

1. Go to bed early, get up early, and be cheerful.
2. Be properly and neatly dressed.
3. Try to get acquainted with your surroundings quickly.
4. Pay attention to your safety and security, and follow instructions and regulations.
5. Ask someone before you start the work if you don't know it well.

This isn't all. There is also a "Three Don'ts" campaign: "Don't do careless things yourself, don't let others do them, don't let accidents happen." The leaders stress that everyone must work with those three points always in mind. It reminds me of the famous proverb: "See no evil, hear no evil, speak no evil." According to the instructor, there were 878 accidents among the 40,000 workers in 1971.

Before lunch, we receive a uniform with the Toyota logo on it and a cap with two green stripes. The two green stripes stand for Seasonal Worker; one green stripe, Probationer; one white stripe, Trainee; one red stripe, Minor; a cap without any stripe, Regular Worker; two yellow stripes, Team Chief; a thick yellow stripe, Foreman; a black stripe on a white cap, General Foreman; a green cap, workers from subcontractors. There are so many ranks that I can't memorize them all at once. It's as if we've joined the army!

After everyone has received a uniform, we go to have our photographs taken. As I sit in front of the camera holding a rectangular piece of cardboard with my registration number on it, I feel like a prisoner. When the company issued me my registration number, it also informed me that the number would be used instead of my name for all company business. I hold a card with 8818639 written on it with a felt-tipped pen. Thus, I am formally hired as a seasonal worker by the Toyota Motor Company.

This evening, orientation finished, we are assigned to various positions. Thirty-seven men have been hired, and out of those thirty-seven, eight have had experience as seasonal workers for Toyota. They'll be paid an extra 17 cents per year of experience per day. The daily pay for a worker with no experience is $8.17, so those who worked last year will get $8.34. Kudo and I are assigned, along with six other guys, to work in the Main Plant. Nine others are assigned to the Miyoshi plant, where they manufacture chassis parts, and the last twenty are sent to the Kamigo plant, where they mainly produce castings and machines.

For two days, the instructors have been stressing the difficulty of the work and emphasizing its dangers. I'm beginning to get uneasy and worry that I might at any moment be discharged as unfit for the job. Earlier, I thought that our employment had been decided formally at the interview at the Public Employment Security Office, but I've been nervous since receiving a note in the mail instructing me to "report" to the company. It warned: "In case you are judged unfit as a worker, for physical or other reasons, you will not be employed."

The two days of orientation are over, and we return

to the dormitory to divide up into groups according to our work assignment. The eight of us going to the Main Plant board a small bus with our baggage and drive to the Third Ohbayashi Pleasant Breeze Dormitory. Still not knowing what kind of jobs are actually waiting for us, we are anxious. We all sit in the bus, silently looking out of the windows into the darkness.

"I wonder where I'll be sold," murmurs a man of about fifty who has already worked here four times before. I feel that he has spoken the thoughts of us all. At this moment all we wish is to spend our six months here doing as easy work as possible with little danger and without having an accident.

The bus takes us to yet another bachelors' dormitory. This one is also surrounded by a tall chain-link fence and guarded by a lookout office. It's as if we've simply moved from one prison to another. We borrow blankets, sheets, and a pillow, and are given name tags to pin up on the door. Then we're told to pair off, and each pair is assigned a room. My roommate is Kudo. It's clever of the company to make men from the same home town share rooms. It helps them adjust to the new environment and stay put during the employment period.

Our room is number 1407. The number means: first building, fourth floor, room number 7. The dormitory supervisors are mostly former Self-Defense Forces men. The dormitories are four-story buildings set in rows. Four people are housed in each two-room apartment. In the center of the dormitory are a dining room, a bath, a social room with a television set, and a small meeting room. Our dormitory accommodates 1,344 men. An identical building facing our dorm with a fence in between—the Refreshing Breeze Dormitory

—holds 2,528 men. In these two dormitories nearly 4,000 men are living. Four thousand young men! It's enough to make me feel dizzy.

Kudo and I carry our blankets and belongings into the vacant room. Then we head out to get a can of beer each at a vending machine. We bring the beers back and drink them in our new room. Kudo earnestly wants to become a regular worker and seems to take it for granted that he'll be one. He talks as though he is one already:

"Think they'll let us live here when I'm married? I wonder if they'll pay a marriage allowance?" He bubbles over with plans for his future as we settle in. "I'll put the color TV here when I buy it."

A little later, Miyamoto, who has been living alone in the next room, returns and comes into our room. Seeing us stubbing out our cigarette butts in an empty beer can, he goes back to his room and brings his own small ashtray.

"The work isn't easy anywhere," he says, "but you'll get used to it soon. So, you're from up north? Ask me about anything you don't understand."

He's from Gifu Prefecture. He's been working here seven or eight years—ever since he graduated.

Friday, September 15

This morning we gather at 7:40 in front of the dormitory office and take the bus to the Main Plant. At the Head Office, we get a mimeographed pamphlet entitled "To All Newcomers." It briefly explains the functions and locations of the various shops in the plant and the automobile production process. We are also advised not to sit up too late in the evening or drink too much.

This plant is as old as the company itself, which was founded in 1938. Here we produce different types of trucks, such as Toyoaces, High Aces, Stouts, and Dyanas, process raw materials by forge, cast and press, assemble engines and chassises, and do final assembly. We also send engines, frames, and gears for passenger cars to many factories where they are needed.

We have to wait in the office until each of our positions is decided. While we wait, we talk a little about our experiences and speculate anxiously about our future work. After we've waited for an hour, they finally begin to call the names, one by one. Kudo and I are called at the same time and are introduced to the section manager. As soon as we enter the room, he says, "I've been waiting for you for a long time." He looks relieved that he's got us at last. My position is Squad 233, the Fifth Machine Plant. My job is to assemble transmissions.

"Can I do it without experience?"

"You'll learn soon enough."

The general foreman is called in, and I'm introduced. The section manager, who has been reading my dossier, speaks reassuringly to the general foreman: "He's thirty-four, so he'll be able to do anything." A peculiar way to guarantee someone's ability.

It's raining. I follow the general foreman to the plant in silence. He leads me into the semidarkness of a disorderly shop. I'm introduced to the foreman, a small man wearing a dirty pair of work pants. He looks good-natured. When I tell him that I'm from Hirosaki, he smiles, wrinkling up the corners of his eyes, and says, "Hirosaki, eh?" He tells me that thirty years ago he was drafted into the Hirosaki regiment. I'm glad it turns out he has good memories of my home town.

It's already afternoon, so I go to the canteen alone. The rush hour is over, and I eat in a leisurely manner. But the self-service system is so complicated that I forget to take something and have to do it all over again. The meal—a bowl of rice and a couple of dishes of fish and vegetables—is cheap, all right, 17 cents a dish, but it's also poorly cooked and tastes awful. There are twenty-three canteens in the plant and twenty-eight dining rooms in the dormitories. Between 1,300,000 and 1,400,000 meals have to be cooked each month. You can't really blame the cooks. All the same, my heart sinks at the prospect of eating here for six months.

When I return from the canteen, the foreman is waiting for me. He shows me around the shop and along the assembly line. "Take it easy today," he says. "It's your first day." I've visited Toshiba and Sony factories, which have assembly lines for televisions and tape recorders, but this is the first time I've seen automobile assembly. The inside of the shop is dirty, noisy, disorderly, and very dim—quite different from the electrical appliance factories. The foreman explains various things to me, but I can barely hear him over the noise. I'm missing half of what he's telling me. I do hear him say that somebody had his third finger stuck and chopped off in a machine yesterday. The family of the injured man was very upset since he was not yet married. He also tells me that a university graduate has been here for a week's practical training. He was so exhausted by the heavy work that he barely lived through the week. The foreman leaves me there alone, saying, "Watch carefully, this might be where you start working tomorrow." But soon the team chief appears and shouts at me, "Hey, you! C'mere!"

The foreman has left me at the beginning of the assembly line, near piles of parts and machines. However, the team chief—a small, pale man about thirty, wearing a belt holding cutting pliers and screwdrivers —takes me to the middle of the line, under a red tin No Smoking sign. "Here's your position."

The men in this area are all young and working briskly. All I can see is that my work looks as if I will be knocking something with a hammer and fastening bolts with the tools that are hanging down above me.

The conveyor belt moves rather slowly. For a second or two I calculate and compare the degrees of difficulty of the two jobs. The one the team chief has given me seems more interesting, if only because it is on the assembly line. I stand and watch for a while. Then the team chief comes up and hands me a new pair of working gloves. "Go ahead and try it." Aren't I supposed to take it easy and look around the place on my first day? But I can't very well argue with my boss, so I put on the gloves. At least it feels good to own a spotless new pair of gloves. Transmission boxes on a revolving tray are coming toward me one after another on the conveyor belt. My job is to put a number of different gears in the box and fasten them with bolts. Beside me, a thin guy, about twenty-two or twenty-three years old, is skillfully handling the tools. He tells me how to do the operation. The cap with his name tag on it is torn at the back and is held in place with a piece of wire. I'm put at his position.

Now that I'm on the assembly line myself, the speed of the belt looks completely different. The slowness was entirely imaginary. Before I can fasten even one gear, my body is pulled to the next station. I try my best to hurry, but it's impossible. I struggle, I fumble —the line never stops. Then I find myself intruding on the next guy's area. While I'm working on only one of the many gears, the next box is already waiting, carried there by the conveyor without my noticing. The young man who taught me the work motions comes running to my rescue. "You'll learn. Don't worry. But it won't be easy to keep up with the speed." Well, he's doing it himself, isn't he? Why not me? I'll do my best. I'll learn. After a while, though, I have a very strange experience. Staring at a box moving steadily by, I suddenly think I see it moving backward.

At night, when I get back to the dorm, Kudo joins me and together we set off for dinner. He has been sent to the drive-shaft shop but not positioned at any particular job yet. There was an accident in his shop today: a man lost three fingers. The general foreman and the foreman were summoned to attend to the matter and didn't return until the end of the day.

We walk back to our room talking about the day's experiences. Miyamoto, who lives in the next room, drops in.

"How did things go?" he asks. When I tell him how I had to struggle to keep up with the speed of the line, he gives me a useful piece of information: "Try to grab as many parts as possible with both hands in one motion. That's the trick of the whole thing. And another thing, you'd better believe that yours is the easiest job. You'll be depressed as hell if you don't."

Today is a day off for the whole company. Looking from the fourth floor, I can see the parking lot below. Rows of Toyota-built cars are parked as though they were in an exhibition. The narrow spaces between them are always crowded with other moving cars. All of them are owned by the residents of the dormitories, most of whom are unmarried and in their twenties. One out of every two workers has a car, of which he made at least a part or two himself. A wire-mesh fence topped with barbed wire forms a square that surrounds buildings, cars, and people as if protecting them. A notice on the fence reads: "Notices or bulletins without permission will be taken down. The company." Another notice in front of the gate says: "For non-residents, an office admission is needed to enter the building." The loudspeaker blares incessantly: "Mr. X of room number xx, you have a visitor." Visitors, whether families or friends, can't enter the dormitory freely; they must have permission.

The dormitory sits between rice fields. The fields in front of the dormitory have already been cut, and the street beside these leveled fields is dotted with a few shops—a laundry, a tailor, a raw-fish restaurant, a pharmacy, an electrical appliance store, a pinball parlor, a bakery, and a restaurant—which cater mostly to the dormitory residents.

Kudo and I had planned to go and have a look around "Toyota City." Because the buses run only once an hour, we decided to make the twenty-minute walk to the Toyota railroad station. There the timetable said that trains also run only once an hour. Disappointed, we waited for the bus. I had imagined that a station near a big company would have some kind of plaza in front, with shops and stores near by. But not this one. The station building is small and isolated—a tiny barracks-like tobacco shop and a telephone booth are all there is to see.

Transportation being what it is, it takes half a day to go anywhere. Toyota calls this town a "city," and in fact, cars are everywhere. The factory vomits cars incessantly. Every store has a parking lot. But for those of us without cars, this town might be deep in the mountains. We couldn't be more isolated. Looking out the bus window, I saw a big placard saying "No admittance except on business." A strange town . . .

Toyota appears so much like a small country town that you'd never guess it has a population of 220,000. There are stores only on the short stretch of the street in front of the station. You can cover the whole town in fifteen minutes.

"Hirosaki is more exciting and more interesting," Kudo said. He looked happy as he remembered our home town.

Sunday, September 17

Kudo has come back with an armful of weekly magazines. He cuts out some photos and pins them up on the wall on his side of the room.

When we were interviewed in Hirosaki, Kudo was wearing his hair rather long, which made the interviewer ask him, "Are you interested in politics?" One glance at his astonished expression was enough to tell me that he couldn't care less about politics. After graduating from the same junior high school I did, he entered the carpentry class of a public vocational training center. The fact that his grandfather was a skilled plasterer must have been partly responsible for that. His father, who worked for the National Railroads was a heavy drinker. He would come back from work drunk, then drink even more. Often, he would get violent. "He was a good Pa when he was sober. He's been dead five years now. He was on the verge of retirement when he died. If he had lived a little longer, Ma would have been able to live more comfortably on his pension." This was his only comment on his father.

When Kudo finished at the vocational training center, he went to work at a carpentry shop in Hirosaki. After a year he went to Saitama Prefecture and became an apprentice under an acquaintance, a carpenter who made Buddhist family altars. When they were pressed with orders, they would work twenty-four hours a day for three or four days running. At the end of his third year, his pay was $100 a month. Last August, he ran into a telephone pole on a motor bike and sustained serious internal injuries and a fractured skull. He was carried unconscious to a hospital in Tokyo. He stayed there a month, and then, when the hospital in Tokyo was closed down, had to go back to a university hospital in Hirosaki. Because of the aftereffects of the head injury, he has been in and out of hospitals ever since. This may explain why he has dark circles under his eyes. He looks old for his age. Though he's cheerful by nature, once in a while a fleeting, sorrowful expression crosses his face. It worries me. He's so good-natured that he doesn't think of himself as unlucky. He even says he's glad he had the accident because it let him quit his apprentice job. He tells me jokingly that at least his family will get a good deal on his altar if he dies.

Monday, September 18

My first workday. Up at 5:00 A.M. It's still dark when I go out. The eastern mountains are glowing faintly, but I can still see the stars shining brightly in the sky. The street is lit by a few scattered lamps. It's a forty-minute walk to the factory. Unfortunately, the plant I have to work in is at the farthest corner of the factory compound. I can't find the canteen and miss breakfast.

I have really been fooled by the seeming slowness of the conveyor belt. No one can understand how it works without experiencing it. Almost as soon as I begin, I am dripping with sweat. Somehow, I learn the order of the work motions, but I'm totally unable to keep up with the speed of the line. My work gloves make it difficult to grab as many tiny bolts as I need, and how many precious seconds do I waste doing just that? I do my best, but I can barely finish one gear box out of three within the fixed length of time. If a different-model transmission comes along, it's simply beyond my capacity. Some skill is needed, and a new hand like me can't do it alone. I'm thirsty as hell, but workers can neither smoke nor drink water. Going to the toilet is out of the question. Who could have invented a system like this? It's designed to make workers do nothing *but* work and to prevent any kind of rest. Yet the man beside me the other day deftly handled his hammer, put the bolts into their grooves with both hands, and fastened them with a nut runner (a power screwdriver that can tighten six bolts simultaneously), seemingly with no difficulty.

The conveyor starts at 6:00 A.M. and doesn't stop until 11:00 A.M. One box of transmissions arrives on the conveyor belt every minute and twenty seconds with unerring precision. When the line stops at eleven o'clock, we tear off our gloves and leave our positions as quickly as we can. We wash our greasy hands and run to the toilet, then rush to the canteen about a hundred yards away where we wait in another line to get our food. After standing five hours, my legs are numb and stiff. My new safety shoes are so heavy that I feel I can barely move. I put my ticket into a box, take an aluminum tray, a pair of chopsticks, a plate of food, a tea cup, and a bowl of rice. I'm still unfamiliar with the routine and have a hard time finding a seat at one of the long tables. Finally, just as I'm settling down to eat, I have the sensation that the trays on the table are moving slowly sideways as if they're on a conveyor belt! At 11:45, the line starts again. There's not much time to rest since ten minutes before work starts we have to begin preparing a large enough supply of parts for the afternoon assemblage.

Above the line, a little to my right, there's a big electric display panel. Under the words "Transmission Assembly Conveyor," there are numbers from 1 to 15. When it is absolutely impossible to catch up with the conveyor, you have to push a button under the belt. This lights up your number in yellow on the board. To halt the line in an emergency, you have to push another button, which triggers a red light and stops the line. Although there are fifteen buttons on the line, there are now only eight workers. To increase production, Toyota decided to use two shifts starting this month. September is the beginning of the high-demand season, and I'm in the first group of seasonal workers hired under this new schedule.

The first shift ends at 2:15 P.M. Already, the man

on the next shift is standing beside me, waiting for me to finish. As soon as I put my hammer down on the belt, he picks it up and begins precisely where I left off. A baton pass, and neatly done, too.

Still, it turns out I'm not finished! I have to spend thirty more minutes replenishing the supply parts for the afternoon shift. I also have to pick up the parts I've scattered on the floor. Damn! My legs ache the entire forty-minute walk back to the dorm. I'm bone tired. Is this the life for a worker in a great enterprise, a famous auto company, proud of being tops in Japan and the third in the world? Somehow I'll have to get used to it.

Tonight Kudo, who had left at eight in the morning, comes back a little after seven. He also had to work two hours overtime. For some reason, the lights in the dorms have gone out. It's really depressing to return to a dark room after walking all the way from the plant.

Kudo is lying spread-eagled on the mat floor. "I didn't quite expect the work to be so hard," he says. Still, he tells me somewhat proudly that he's made 400 pieces today. I don't know how many I made myself, or for that matter, don't really know what I was making. Exactly what part of the gear box were they? I was much too busy to look at the other guys' operations. I didn't even have time to look at my watch. After a while, I felt like I was making some part of a child's plastic toy. What was I really doing? The sign in my shop has a word for it—"Assembly"!

Tonight, I'm too tired to sleep and awfully nervous about having to get up early tomorrow. I get up and go out to buy a can of beer. A picture of Ken Takakura, a famous actor, smiles down at me from the vending machine. Even beer is sold by machines.

When I return, I hear Kudo muttering to himself in his bed, "I wish I'd been killed in that accident. It would have been much easier to die while I was unconscious."

Tuesday, September 19

As I walked to work this morning, I noticed that the sun rose a little later. The glow around the edges of the mountains was thinner than yesterday.

The work, though, was the same plus overtime for an hour. Now that I'm back in my room it's hard to believe that I've stood there working for nine hours. At times, my head was spinning. The work is still very hard, and all day I found myself crowding the next guy's position. Once I fall behind the line pace, I'm unable to get back to my regular position. Though I double my efforts, using twice as much energy, I just can't recover the lost seconds. It's like I imagine hell to be.

Once, when I saw Chaplin's *Modern Times*, I remember really laughing at his accelerated motions as he tried to keep up with the line. But I won't laugh any more—I'm doing the same thing now. All day, the boxes arrive at a fixed speed and at regular intervals with mechanical precision. The line is a machine, and for eight hours the humans working at it are required to operate with machinelike accuracy. The line demands speed—relentless, mechanical, and unchanging.

The term "conveyor belt" suggests automation, but actually the work is done by human hands. Only the parts are transferred by automatic power. The first worker, standing at the beginning of the assembly line, feeds the conveyor with parts. The next person assembles the parts, and the man next to him adds still more parts. All this is done in accordance with the line speed. The people working on the line are nothing more than power consumed in the process of assembly. What is achieved at the end of the line is the result of our combined energy. There's no need to shout at or berate workers to make them work. Just start the conveyor and keep it going: that's enough. The conveyor belt forces the workers into submission. During our working hours, we can't even talk. Even if we wanted to chat, the noise is so awful we can't hear one another.

Kudo comes back around six-thirty. He tells me he has been transferred to another job. He has to assemble five or six kinds of parts, and uses safety goggles. He shows me the goggles. He's happy because this job is easier.

"Easy job, I love that," he hums to himself as he goes out to take a bath. He comes back with a color TV catalogue and says he is going to buy a set. He'll pay $83 on our first payday, $83 again on our next payday, and the $167 balance when he gets his bonus. I tell him that we won't be paid until the twentieth of next month, and not even for the complete month, only for thirteen or fourteen days work. We'll probably get less than $130. I ask him how he is going to eat after he has paid for his luxury.

"Well, I'll only pay five or ten dollars at first." He isn't at all discouraged. "I think I'll buy a small heater. There's an outlet, so I'll put it here, and the TV there." He talks as if he's already a regular worker. Cars keep driving between the dorm buildings until midnight.

Wednesday, September 20

Bad luck that my room is on the fourth floor. I curse the stairs every time I see them. After work, I climb the stairs on all fours, stagger to my room, open the door, and fall in, no longer able to stay on my feet. I jogged all spring to prepare myself, but it hasn't helped much. No amount of training can prepare you for this work. During the eleven-hour workday (I leave the dorm at 5:00 A.M. and don't return until 4:00 P.M.) there is only forty-five minutes for rest. Nine hours labor and an hour and a half walking to and from the plant. My back aches from bending down to reach the old-style conveyor belt. My right wrist aches, too, from swinging a hammer all day. My right arm muscles are swollen. It's true I'm now able to complete one transmission out of two. But I will still have to work twice as fast to do the job properly, and as long as I can't keep up with the pace of the line, I can't be on an equal footing with my fellow workers.

Today's payday for everyone but us seasonal workers. We aren't paid until the twentieth of next month. Why should a big company like Toyota hold back the payment in this way? There are 41,000 workers getting an average of $300 a month, including overtime wages. That makes $12,300,000 for the company to play with as it wishes.

Late in the afternoon Kudo comes back. "The people who got paid today are buying stuffed dolls out on the street," he says.

We go downstairs. There, by the road in front of the dormitory, a man is selling big stuffed animals. The men who buy them put them beside the drivers' seats of their cars.

"What gives? They're all men, aren't they?" I ask.

"And bachelors. They're going to sleep with the dolls."

Thursday, September 21

The weather has been beautiful for days. Life would be unbearable if it rained.

Our lockers are in a prefabricated two-story building resembling a bunkhouse. I put my card into the time puncher: 5:50. Most of the workers are already wearing their work clothes and are sitting smoking cigarettes on the bench in front of their lockers. I've been leaving the dorm with my work clothes on, so all I have to do is put on my safety shoes and work cap. I push the heavy steel workshop door open. Whenever I open it I think to myself, "I'm leaving the world of the living and entering hell."

The team chief has been busy for thirty minutes preparing the line. He's lit all the lamps, so they're ready to go. At 6:00 A.M. the conveyor belt starts. From then on we enter a time without freedom, from this moment until 11:00 A.M.: five hours of work without a break.

One transmission arrives every minute and twenty seconds at five-foot intervals. Until the end of last month it was every fifty seconds. (Then fifteen people worked on one transmission every fifty seconds— seventy per hour.) Now eight people produce one transmission every minute and twenty seconds, or forty-six transmissions per hour. Most workers say they prefer the new arrangement. Work is easier now that the workers have more variety in their tasks. Before, there were more people but the work was far more monotonous, and the pace was faster. Until last month the line was in motion from 8:00 A.M. to 7:00

P.M. Sometimes, though, the line ran until 9:30 P.M., and some people had to work until well past 11:00 at night. This was beyond the limits of human endurance, and workers were quitting. Worried, the management put in the two-shift system. The first shift is from 6:00 A.M. to 2:15 P.M., and the second shift from 2:15 to 11:00 P.M. The daily production quota is 715 transmissions.

Friday, September 22

Starting today, I work alone. The man who had been helping me was transferred to the opposite side of the workshop to feed the conveyor with parts. But I couldn't do the work alone. Whenever I fell behind, crowding the next area, I lit my number on the board. Seeing the yellow light, the team chief would come running. With his help, I'd get back to my original position. Then the team chief would disappear, leaving me alone. In a few minutes I'd find myself in the next area again and I'd have to push the button. The same thing happened again and again. On my fifth day I became an "independent" worker. It usually takes a couple of days for workers to start working alone.

I'm tired. I don't believe anybody could be more tired. Is this what "labor-intensive" means? I never imagined there was labor so "intense" that you couldn't rest even one second. The only consolation is that I smoke less now. One cigarette before work, one before lunch, one after lunch, one just before work begins again in the afternoon, and one when work is over. Five cigarettes at the plant, none during work. In the dormitory I do nothing but sleep. Work should be something that varies, sometimes rushed, sometimes leisurely, with occasional cigarettes and chats with your colleagues. What kind of labor is this? Toyota has designed this job so that a worker can only keep up with the line by always exerting the utmost effort at top speed. For seven and a half hours in the first shift and for eight hours (not including overtime) in the second shift, it's as if you're tied to the conveyor, exhausted and gasping for breath.

The man in front of me, Fukuyama, is past forty and from Kumamoto. He came to Toyota five years ago as a seasonal worker and eventually became a regular. Originally he was a welder in a body plant, but he's been assigned here to help out for the time being. He has been working in our plant for three months now. Even though he arrived a couple of months before I did, sometimes he falls behind and finds himself in my area. Once you've lost a few seconds inserting a part, you can never make them up.

This evening Fukuyama and I were walking side by side toward the canteen when suddenly he said with much emotion, "They're controlling the speed with a computer to match the speed of veteran workers. How can a new worker possibly keep up with it?"

Kudo came back well past eight. He had done an hour of overtime before his regular work and two hours after the shift. "Know something?" he said. "I did 530 pieces today." And then he added, "I'll buy a motorcycle when I become a regular. It's a hell of a long walk to and from the plant."

Saturday, September 23

My slow pace causes a lot of trouble. I still can't manage alone. An automobile inspection delegation from China is scheduled to visit the plant. We wait for them in our transmission section, doing overtime for two hours, but they don't show up.

One week gone. It's been a tough experience. My right hand is blistered and sore from driving the bolts. My back and ribs ache so much I had to buy a compress for them. I wake up each morning with both hands stiff and bent inward, but once the line starts, I grab the hammer, begin hammering, and forget everything, even the pain.

The company paid us our transportation allowance today—the train fare we had to pay to come here from our home towns. Everyone was surprised, for the company had told us they would pay the allowance on October 30, our first payday. The back of the envelope containing the money said "Toyota Consumers' Cooperative," which was strange. Why should money paid by the company be delivered in an envelope of the cooperative, an organization that supposedly is separate from the Toyota management?

Next week I'll work on the afternoon shift. I'm determined to slog through the six months somehow.

Sunday, September 24

The morning paper reports the wedding of a well-known reporter, Junichiro Kuroki, to an actress, Chieko Matsubara. It seems far away, very unreal. I slept twelve hours straight last night. My body's still sore all over. Kudo went to work at 8:00 A.M. for half a day. He left the dormitory grumbling, "Work work work, nothing but work. Know something? It's Sunday, man. And what do I do? Work, that's what. Glad I'm not married. This job's not for men with women."

Kudo tells me of some graffiti on the toilet wall at

his plant: "Twenty years and still no car of my own." True. But it's also true that most of the young workers buy cars on the installment plan. There's practically no amusement near by. You get up in the morning, walk to the plant, work, come back, take a bath, eat, and go to bed. That's what "life" at Toyota is all about.

Daizo Kusayanagi, a famous writer-critic, wrote this about Toyota life:

> The rice is cooked instantly in a vacuum cooker. After eating this rice, the workers go to work in the plant. And when they have finished work, they go back to their dormitories, which are well equipped with modern facilities and have cost the company $200 million. . . . Toyota Motor Company is trying to create human beings, too. I was fascinated and much impressed by this "Great Country Town" after the complete tour of the company.*

He was telling the truth, of course, but there is so much that he didn't tell about. He should have written this:

> The rice served here is bad for the digestion because it's cooked too fast. The workers eat the rice in a hurry, go to the plant in a hurry, and work in a hurry in order to keep up with the "famous" assembly line. After they are finally released, they have no choice other than to go back to the dormitories, which have facilities that are advertised by the Public Relations Department to have cost the company $200 million.

---

* *The Enterprise as Kingdom* (Tokyo: Bungei-Shunju Co., 1969), p. 174.

There, former Self-Defense Forces men now working for Toyota keep a close eye on everyone's private lives.

Monday, September 25

I'm on the second shift this week and went to the plant in the afternoon.

Last night, I lay awake a long time, and when I finally fell asleep, I dreamed I held a gear in my left hand and a shaft in my right. I was trying to put the gear into a transmission case, trying to fasten the shaft with a bolt. But the shaft wouldn't go in, and I had to finish the procedure in ten seconds. The line continued moving while I was struggling with the shaft. I came out of the dream for a moment and went back to sleep again. Then the same nightmare returned. It kept going like that. I probably slept for no more than four hours.

I still can't manage alone on the line. Today the team chief rushed over and admonished me, "Move your hands fast!"

Why does everyone work at this goddamn job without complaining? Incredibly, thirty minutes before the second shift, everybody is always ready. They change clothes unhurriedly, begin preparing the parts they'll use in their work, and five minutes before their own shift they're already working with the guys on the other shift. They're so docile and undoubting that I could almost cry. Whenever we meet, Kudo and I look at each other, sigh, and say, "Long day." "Yeah, long as hell." It's only two weeks since I left home, but I feel it's been two or three months. Kudo agrees with me. The job's that bad. Kudo's working now from

8:00 P.M. to 7:00 A.M. with only one hour's break. Yesterday morning, he came back from work with a cut an inch long beside his left eye. He had been hit in the face by a drive shaft that was being carried on a trolley conveyor. He couldn't have it treated. Not even first aid.

I wonder how the regular workers take the situation? What do they think of their union? Every day they go straight home in their cars. They never seem to get together and talk among themselves over drinks, or over anything, for that matter.

Thursday, September 28

I went to take a bath downstairs this morning. When I came out, my wooden clogs were gone. You're not often robbed these days, even in public baths. When I went to the dining room, there was nothing left to eat. Here every day is a small war.

There is a Safety First meeting ten minutes before the shift begins. It's not fair for management to force a meeting on the workers during their off time, but no one protests.

There are some complaints among the workers. When the company declared an increase in output, it promised that ten workers from another plant would be sent here as reinforcements. In the end, only eight came. The only way not to hold up the line was to off-set the labor shortage by working overtime. Workers are angry.

"What we can't do, we can't do," one worker says. "The company should be satisfied."

"If we really care about Safety First," another says, "why don't they hire more workers? That's top priority."

But still, when the time comes, we all return to work without protest. By 10:00 P.M. everyone is exhausted. It is all I can do to keep my hands in motion on the line. But strangely, time passes and the line moves on, and somehow each day's work ends.

I'm responsible for assembling two kinds of truck transmissions, and by now I can do about 90 percent of the required work. I'd give anything just to keep up with the murderous conveyor. I hate having to push the button to call the team chief and reveal my incompetence again and again.

Takeda, whose position is next to mine, helps me sometimes by rushing through his own work to give me a whole minute of his precious time. "Tell me how to do it and I'll help you. My job is simple. I can spare the minute."

I know he really can't spare the minute. Nobody on the line can afford the luxury of helping others. I am touched.

But there's another side to Takeda's generosity. He's dying from the monotony of his own work. I'm thankful for his help, of course, but Takeda also wants to try something new and strange, something that breaks the deadly boredom, the relentless repetition of the assembly line. There, where no amount of intelligence, creativity, or freedom is permitted, he can release some tension and refresh his energy by helping me, and that helps him get through the day.

Almost all the workers here are hard-working. In most factories, there are those who work very hard and those who don't. But here, the conveyor-belt system makes everyone work at exactly the same pace. Even off the line, we all begin preparing parts even before our shift starts, time which is still our supper break, for without this preparation we'd never get the work done.

It is raining when work finishes. I am depressed, already worrying if I will make it through to next February, when my contract expires. Takeda asks Yoshizaki, who happens to live near my dorm, to give me a lift.

The joint at the base of my right third finger is numb. I can't bend it at all.

Friday, September 29

As soon as he got back this morning, Kudo said in a tired voice, "Guess what? I got transferred again." Until suppertime, he said, he'd been doing the same work as he did the day before. Then, they changed his position.

"It's outrageous. This is the seventh time they've changed my position. What do they think I am?"

Even good-natured Kudo got angry! The job they've given him has caused two fatal accidents. Last year, and also three years ago, seasonal workers were killed as they turned a drive shaft during testing. The shaft, weighing over 130 pounds, spun out of the machine and into the workers.

"I could be the third. But why worry? My family can buy my altar cheap. Lucky, huh?" He tried to laugh it all off, without much success. He is not going to work tonight. He doesn't have the strength.

I'm tired at work, too. One hour's work and my back's breaking. A week's exhaustion piled up.

"We'll only do 330 boxes today," the team chief says. "Let's take it easy for a change. We'll finish at ten-thirty. "There'll be a meeting after that."

We're glad to hear the news, but the conveyor doesn't stop until 10:45, only fifteen minutes before the regular time. We're happy, though, because we don't have to do the usual overtime. Once again, the topic at the meeting is "Safety." Sugimoto, who's about twenty-two, says, "We can't stand up straight after ten hours on our legs. It's natural there are accidents when we try to do that work when we're exhausted."

We all silently agree with him, but most of us are too tired to say anything and just sit there on the bench.

Finally, someone hoots at the team chief, "Write down what he said just now, will you?" But generally there's an air of resignation. Workers feel that nothing they say will reach the top.

Yoshizaki again offers me a ride back to the dormitory. He's twenty-seven, from Kagoshima, with thick eyebrows and big eyes. He doesn't talk much, though I do know he came to Toyota from the Self-Defense Forces. He's been with Toyota for seven years now, and last April he was "rotated" from the Miyoshi plant.

Saturday, September 30
People on the second shift have Saturdays off. I stayed in bed all day. The *Toyota*, the company paper, quoted a survey conducted by the Japan Automobile Manufacturers' Association citing the August output of the two biggest automobile companies in Japan:

Toyota   132,535 vehicles
Nissan   127,122 vehicles
(Gap: 5,413 vehicles)

Another headline read: "Toyota to Put More Emphasis on Pollution Control and Safety Measures. Investments Due to Reach $155 Million."

But after reading the article carefully, I realized the increase in money would be used for plant and equipment and overseas investment. The article ended by stating: "We expect that this increase of capital will contribute to strengthening the production structure for 'TOYOTA—Cars to Love'."

2

HOW NEW RECORDS ARE MADE

Sunday, October 1

This evening in the canteen I meet Yamamoto, who's from Kurume in northern Kyushu. We chat for a while after dinner. At first, after graduating from commercial high school three years ago, he wanted to go to college, but gave up the idea because he had no father and figured the quickest way to earn and save money was to become a seasonal worker instead of joining a company. That was three years ago. He's a pleasant man, well-mannered, neat.

Here at Toyota, he now grinds engine cylinder blocks. He worked at several plants before he came here, including a Celica assembly line at Toyota's Takaoka plant, a machinery plant at Kamigo, a Datsun forging plant in Yokohama, and a Kubota power-shovel assembly line in Osaka.

"Look how yellow my hands are!" he says, frowning. "I scrubbed them with a brush, but they're still yellow. I hate this crap." He tells me how his shirts, pants, and hair are always coated with powder from cast metals. He's trying to endure his job by just concentrating on his next payday, when he'll decide whether to stay here or quit for good although his contract lasts until the end of this year. His chief hope is that he'll be able to put up with his job until the end of his contract. That way he could save some money and return to start a new life—a life in a white shirt and tie.

I've been working two weeks now. When I come back from work, I do nothing but sleep. I try not to think about the job; even the thought of it is enough to make me feel sick. Mostly, I feel too tired to think about anything.

I still fall behind at work. As soon as I push the alarm button, my team chief runs up to me and asks in a disgusted tone, "Haven't you learned yet? Watch closely—I'll show you one more time." Then he goes through the operation slowly and condescendingly. At a crucial point, he looks at me and says, "See? Do it like this. Haven't you learned yet?" At first I was shocked, but then I realized that here at Toyota "to learn" means merely to acquire the ability to keep up with the line, quickly repeating certain physical movements while thinking absolutely nothing.

Each individual worker has his own way of working and should be entitled to produce goods in his own way. There should be a variety of working methods. But in fact, there is only one method of producing goods in the fastest possible way: standardized work. If we don't make the precise motions we're "taught," it's absolutely impossible to do the required work in the required time. Under such a system, all our movements must become mechanical and habitual. Only if we stop thinking and unconsciously follow this system can we keep up. Our bodies are treated just as if they were machines. As a couple of other workers once told me, "Once you're used to the job, you can do it sleeping." At that point, we've literally become parts of the machine.

Broken down, these are my movements working on models KM and PH:

1. I pick up two knock pins (small pieces of steel shaft) with my left hand from a parts box (where identical parts are stored) in front of the assembly line. I insert them into the upper holes on a gear box and then knock them in with the hammer in my right hand.

2. With my right hand, I take an input shaft out of a tin box coming down the assembly line. I insert it into the center hole of the gear box. Holding the input shaft from the other side with my left hand, I drive it in with the hammer. (Sometimes it doesn't go in easily.)

3. With my left hand, I screw a synchronizing ring to an end into which an input shaft has been driven.

4. I turn the gear box around.

5. With my left hand, I take out a reverse idler gear from the tin box. I put it into the gear box and press it with my hand. With my right hand I take a shaft out of the parts box and insert it into a hole on the opposite side of the gear box. I insert the shaft through the idler hole and then fit it into the gear box. With my right hand I pick up a small semicircular pin (it's hard with gloves on) and force it into a slot on the shaft to connect it to the gear box. (The pointed end of the shaft doesn't always go smoothly into the hole in the gear box.)

6. The line brings an output shaft (which has many gears) placed upright in a hole in the gear box. I lift it with both hands and place it horizontally into the gear box. Then I connect it to the input shaft that I put in previously and fix them in their correct position in a slot so that they rotate freely.

7. With my left hand I reach over to a box on the other side of the line to get a molded metal fork.

With my right hand I take a hub out of the tin box. I connect the parts at two places, using two clips that I've picked up with my right hand (very difficult with gloves on!).

8. With my left hand I pick up a bearing lock from the tin box. Then I turn around. I place the bearing lock on top of a line mount. I pick up a rubber oil seal and put it into a hole in the bearing lock. Pressing the oil seal with a cold-chisel-shaped stick in my left hand, I hammer the oil seal in. (If I bend the oil seal, the transmission will leak oil.)

9. After hammering the oil seal in, I take out a paper gasket that's hanging down in front of my eyes. I soak it in liquid bond and then apply it to the rim of the bearing lock.

10. I turn around again and face the line and put the bearing lock on it. I grab the hammer and start doing step 1 again. In all, I assemble fifteen big and small parts. More than two-thirds of the transmissions I and others assemble here are models KM and PH. Most of these transmissions are shipped to the Toyota Auto Body Company, a subsidiary truck-chassis assembly plant.

My movements working on models RY and RK are only slightly different. Since transmissions of this type have many attached parts, workers are literally gasping for breath if ten of them come down the line in a row.

Tuesday, October 3
Overtime for an hour. I come back with Takeda, who works next to me. He's only nineteen and from Shizuoka Prefecture. After finishing ninth grade, he was hired as a trainee. For three years, he went to Toyota's Voca-

tional High School while he worked at the factory. After graduation two years ago, he was able to get assigned to the maintenance section. He liked the job there, since he could learn a lot about different machines and had some free time when there were no machines to repair. But he often had to work on Sundays, which interfered with the mountain-climbing club activities in which he was becoming interested. So he applied for work in a shop where he could take Sundays off. He was transferred to this transmission plant in March.

Suddenly he says, "This job's dull, don't you think?" Dull as hell, all right, but I'm surprised that he's so outspoken. He's a regular Toyota employee, a Toyota Vocational High School graduate who is supposed to be eligible to become a team chief faster than others. Besides, he's a quiet guy who rarely talks to his fellow workers at the plant.

We go to the co-op store together and kill time looking at books and shirts. When the canteen opens at four, he goes on for supper. I head for the bus stop in front of the pinball parlor, then wait on the river bank for the bus.

I'm so worn out I feel numb all over. As soon as I return to the dorm I spread out my bedding, lie down, and read a newspaper. But I can't stop myself from falling asleep. I wake up an hour later and go to the bath, where I massage my stiff wrists and fingers. Then I walk to the dining room on the second floor, have a glass of tomato juice with dinner, and lie down on the bed again. After eight I go out to get a can of beer from a vending machine, come back, and fall on my bed. I get up at 5:00 A.M. again. This is my exciting everyday life when I'm on the first shift! It's becoming almost as mechanical as my job. Sensations move monotonously by me like parts on a conveyor.

Kudo's now working from eight in the morning to seven in the evening. Before he worked from seven to seven, including three hours of overtime. Though his overtime work has been cut to two-and-a-half hours, his position is still the same—as dangerous as before. He asked the team chief for a transfer. "But why?" the team chief asked. "You're a temporary worker! You're here to earn money, aren't you? Stick to it. Don't worry, you won't be here long." ("Temporary workers" is what the regular employees call us. It describes our status more accurately than "seasonal workers.")

Tuesday, October 4

The *Chunichi Daily* has an article called "Air Pollution: Automobiles Are Main Offenders."

> In March the Environmental Protection Agency made public the results of a survey which reveal that among air-polluting gases, 93 percent of carbon monoxide, 57 percent of hydrocarbon, and 39 percent of nitrogen oxide come from car exhaust! The survey tried to determine how much air pollution has been caused by cars now that the United States' clean air standards are being introduced in Japan. An agency committee investigated the amounts of carbon oxide, hydrocarbons, and nitrogen oxide given off by automobiles, power plants, and the chemical and petrochemical industries.

Another article in the paper says that the Central Council for Environmental Pollution Control submitted a Japanese draft of the U.S. Emission Control Law to Osanori Koyama, director general of the Environmental Protection Agency. Automobiles have now been proved to be the main air-pollution offenders, yet every day and every minute these offenders flow out of automobile plants and run around cities as if they owned them.

Thursday, October 5

A meeting after work. Mostly, we talk about our section manager's new order to check the tightness of all six bolts in the transmission. It's impossible for us to add one more operation. We're already too pressed for time. The team chief tries to force it on us, using the oldest excuse in the world:

"It's an order from the section manager."

One worker answers coldly, "Well, if it's an order, it's an order. But the line's going to stop."

"I don't care. Let it stop."

"You say you don't care? But the people on the second shift will have to work overtime to make up for us."

Another worker exclaims, "They'll have to work until two or three o'clock in the morning! That's impossible. What sort of people do the management think we are?"

Everybody starts complaining all at once. Finally, the general foreman, a stout man with a white cap, proposes a compromise: "Well, we'll try measuring at only one point. I'll ask the management about it."

"One place is plenty!" someone shouts in disgust.

Suddenly the section manager, who issued the order, comes in. He's still young, about forty. The general foreman tells us rather ceremoniously, "Please pay special attention to safety." Then he stands and leaves in spite of our anger. The meeting has "ended." We also stand and leave the narrow locker room. As we're filing out, someone tells the section manager, "You've got to think more about us," but the words no longer have an icy edge. They're more like a joke. Even the experienced workers are getting upset. I'm relieved to know that others are as discontented as I am.

Friday, October 6

Work still leaves me stiff and sore. The joints of my right hand and wrist ache so much that I'm applying compresses to them and to my left thumb, plus one on the right side of my back. Every day I have to massage the sore places and warm them in the bath in order to keep on working. One day when we changed shifts, the team chief of the other shift smelled the compresses as he passed by. "My God," he teased, "you're falling apart already, aren't you?" In spite of all those sore parts, I can handle the models PH and KM almost by myself, since they have no covers to be adjusted.

I am reminded of an American movie called *The Defiant Ones*. In it, a white and a black prisoner handcuffed to each other try to escape. They hate each other, but they've been put in a situation where they have to cooperate in order to escape. Much like that, if Fukuyama, the worker on my right, falls behind, he'll pull me behind, since I barely keep up with the work myself. Even if Fukuyama finishes his job in time, should I take longer on my job, then the next worker, Takeda, will be pulled out of his position. It takes enormous energy to catch up with the line, and if things go wrong, the line stops. That means overtime. So we do our job in a hell of a hurry to keep our fellow workers from suffering. That is how Toyota raises output.

As I'm about to leave the workshop, my general

foreman approaches me smiling. He looks closely into my face and asks, "How are you doing? Do you think you'll be OK?"

"Yes, I'll catch up with the line soon."

"Good!" He nods curtly. After a short pause, he reminds me, "Don't take the day off."

My face must look tired, and besides, tomorrow is Saturday. Unreported absenteeism is what supervisors dread most. I simply mention that I haven't received my ID yet. It worries me that I haven't got mine yet while Kudo and the others got theirs more than a week ago.

I come back with Takeda. He lives alone in a small apartment house on the way to my dorm. He says that one day in the workshop, he heard a group that included our team chief talking: "Here, at this position, we have five unused seconds." The speed of the line is determined by stopwatch! He also tells me that the torque measurement of the six bolts, which made everyone so angry at yesterday's meeting, was originally scheduled to be my work. But they found I couldn't handle it, so they gave it to him. Then they found he couldn't do it either, so it was finally forced on the inspectors at the end of the line.

Saturday, October 7

There's a new graffito on a toilet wall: "I'm only in it for the money." On first thought that seems like common sense. But it started me thinking. Could it be a kind of protest against hard, monotonous work without any future? Though workers aren't satisfied just to receive money, or at least don't like to admit they are, the actual work is a simple exchange of labor for money. The graffito seems to be saying that since that's all our labor is, we want at least to declare that we are the masters of our own life during our free time. Or am I reading too much into this graffito? Kudo, for example, seems to take it for granted that work is by nature a painful thing. He doesn't criticize it and tells himself that it doesn't really matter what the work is like. He got hit on the face and then later hurt his fingers badly with a hammer. A machine ripped his shirt and took the buttons off, sparks from an electric welder burned holes all over his shirt, and grease has completely ruined his pants, yet he doesn't complain much.

Yesterday at his shop, they found they had produced a hundred defective drive shafts. Something went wrong with the machines that make them. Kudo told me angrily that it happened because the machines are old and the team chief doesn't maintain them well enough. What will happen to the workers who produced the drive shafts? They repaired sixty of them today, but forty had to be thrown out.

Sunday, October 8

Fine weather. Kudo and I climb up to the dormitory roof. It's covered with so many television antennas that we can hardly walk around. Below us, rice fields spread out to meet the hills. In the distance we can see the chimney of the plant where we work every day.

As I'm going back upstairs after supper, I run into Yamamoto, who is coming downstairs to take a bath. He tells me how tough his job is. His workshop demands three-and-a-half hours of overtime every day. His foreman and team chief come to the workshop at eight in the morning and leave at nine at night. "It's OK with me, since I'm leaving at the end of this year," he adds as usual. He too has persuaded himself that his hard work is just for money. Kudo, Yamamoto, and I get through our days by counting down the number left until our contracts expire. But what about the regular workers? What are they waiting for?

Sunday, October 9

I'm on the second shift this week. I'm exhausted before I even get started. None of us have the slightest chance of winning the race with the line, of beating this machine. The line stops for the supper break. Before I leave to eat, I take oil seals out of their wrapping paper all alone, preparing for the next job. The foreman approaches and says, "Don't work when you're off. You're not paid for it. Let the team chief do it later." I can tell he isn't saying this as my boss. I've never known him to order us around or yell at us. We all like him, and workers who come to our workshop as temporary reinforcements agree that "The old man's a good guy." But it's also true that if the boss is a nice guy, workers find it hard to get angry or show their discontent.

Yoshizaki gives me a ride back. He has two children.

"Do you go out driving on Sundays?" I ask.

"No. I just stay home, resting."

"Really? Do you get worn out too?"

"Sure." After a short pause, he adds as if talking to himself, "Continually changing shifts is bad news. I only get to see my kids when they're in bed. I'd like to eat with them sometimes."

The *Toyota Weekly* has an article entitled "The General Federation of Japan Automobile Workers' Unions, Our Long-Cherished Desire, Is Finally Formed."

The inaugural convention of the General Federation of Japan Automobile Workers' Unions and its first annual convention were held in Tokyo on October 3 and 4. The former council organization was widened into the General Federation, creating a trade union with 500,000 affiliates. From today, various activities will be carried out under the slogan "Let's make a new industrial union and a welfare society worth living and working in."

Our new automobile union is stressing solidarity after eighteen years of disunity. After the All Japan Auto Workers' Union dissolved in 1954, activities were carried out separately by several groups: Toyota, Isuzu, Hino, and Suzuki formed one group, called the All Japan Federation of Automobile Workers' Unions; Datsun had the Federation of Japan Automobile Workers' Unions; and Mazda, Honda, and Fuji formed separate unions of their own. Today these trade unions were finally reunited. The new union decided to back Takezo Watanabe* in the upcoming national election.

The dissolution of the All Japan Federation of Automobile Workers' Unions, the formation of the Federation of All Toyota Auto Workers' Unions, and the formation of the General Federation of Japan Automobile Workers' Unions—the reorganization of labor organizations—has been a rapid response to the reorganization of the auto industry itself. But the

---

* Takezo Watanabe is a former Toyota employee. Some big companies and their unions jointly support candidates to protect their interest; many of them are from the Democratic Socialist Party, a centrist minority party represented in the national Diet. It advocates compromise between labor and management and often supports the ruling conservative Liberal Democratic Party.

workers here never talk about these issues. Is the "solidarity" of the unions something separate from the workers? The unions still haven't concerned themselves with the reality—the numbing, grueling daily work on the line.

In the December 1972 issue of the *Labor Problems Monthly*, President Shoiji said: "If there aren't any labor unions in countries where we extend our business, we'll try to organize one there. We eventually want to organize an Automobile Manufacturing Industry World Council." But how will the workers in the new economic "colonies" greet union leaders who arrive hand-in-hand with big business?

Tuesday, October 10

Three hours is still the limit I can work without stopping. But it's a five-hour stretch until our meal breaks. Why can't we have a short break in between? I'd love to bang my hammer on the line and storm out shouting, "Go to hell!" What do the other workers think of this monotonous work as they repeat it in cycles of a minute and twenty seconds? I asked Takeda what goes through his mind at work. He looked a bit surprised, but quickly replied, "Time, I guess." Me too. All I think of is time. I think: I've worked one hour . . . now two hours . . . four hours more to go . . . three-and-a-half hours more . . . three more hours to go . . . Do I have to work overtime today? . . . Should I do my laundry after work? I can't think of anything else. Sometimes I think of something totally illogical: landscapes with towns I once visited suddenly appear one by one. Perhaps a restaurant beside a bridge, a coffee shop around the corner near a station, a harbor, all of which I haven't seen for years. It's impossible to concentrate on any one scene. How can you contemplate anything serious in a cycle of a minute and twenty seconds? You just have to accept fragments of memories as they race by. Even your unconscious mind starts to mimic the line.

Our work is not to create but to assemble. Knowledge and experience don't make any difference—a fifteen-year-old boy could do the work as well as I. Even if he continued the job for twenty years, until he was my age, his work would leave him without any other knowledge, skill, or power of judgment. The result would still be something that leaves in precisely one minute and twenty seconds.

Around eight in the morning Kudo returned from work. He was pale and his eyes were bloodshot. He'd done two-and-a-half hours overtime. "I'm dead tired. Boy, am I tired!" He often says this, using his home-town accent. He threw himself over his unmade bed, where he fell right asleep in the bright morning sun.

He missed breakfast and will miss lunch, too, since they don't serve lunch in the dorm. He seems too tired to do anything but sleep. He likes cars and came to Toyota hoping that he could help make them. But now he's lost all hope. His job is so tough that it knocks out a young man of only twenty-one. His team chief told him that nobody liked Kudo's present job and warned him not to be absent. "If I don't come," Kudo says, "he has to do my job himself. That's why he asked me to come." These days he doesn't talk about becoming a regular worker any more.

Wednesday, October 11

I worked until midnight with one hour overtime. After that, thirty minutes overtime for cleaning up. As he drove me back home, Yoshizaki told me that in August they often did six hours (!) of overtime: two hours on the line, the rest repairing defective parts.

Thursday, October 12

I've survived another day. It's 1:30 A.M. I just got a real shock when I saw my face in the mirror. Dry skin and dull, bloodshot eyes—it looked inhuman, the face of a loser who pities himself and secretly hates himself for doing so. How long will my aching body hold out? I've lost confidence in myself. I still can't keep up with the line. My life is a sad cycle of getting up, going to the workshop, sleeping, then getting up again and carrying my tired body to the line just in time for it to start moving. Something in me is breaking.

This morning I was smoking on the way to work. About a hundred yards outside the main gate of the plant, there's a surveillance station in the middle of the road to check the cars that pass through. The guards there wear uniforms exactly like policemen. One of them yelled at me to put my cigarette in an ashcan beside the road. I wasn't even inside the plant, but I sheepishly obeyed this unreasonable order—prohibition of smoking on a public road. The only resistance I offered was to click my tongue. If a Tokyo cop had told me to put out my cigarette like that, I would have told him where to go, but here I just obeyed like a sheep. This servile attitude must be written on my face.

Friday, October 13

During the break after supper, the team chief told us that starting next month our production quota would be 760 boxes. We all protested. Everyone was angry.

"We used to have a minute and twenty seconds," someone said. "Now all we'll have is a minute and eighteen seconds. Do you know this?"

"I'll stop work early tonight," someone else said, "and get back my lost time."

"Management told us that they'd send ten more workers, but only eight have arrived."

"Cost reduction, cost reduction. That's all they care about. It's simple. It's been ten years since this plant was built, so the more we work, the more money they'll get."

"They're cutting quality for quantity. They said we would have three inspection machines, but now we have only two."

The team chief listened silently and acted as though he were simply relaying a message from the management. It was infuriating. But no matter how angry we get, we go back to the line, and once the line starts, there is no time to complain. Our anger is always stillborn.

Saturday, October 14

Bright day. Miyamoto, from next door, comes back in the morning after the night shift. Piling some camping gear in his car, he immediately leaves for the mountains. He tells us it will take him five hours by car. Kudo and I are amazed at his toughness. As he leaves he says, "You'll never survive here unless you have a hobby."

Kudo does his wash, singing a Toyota jingle: "The young people at Toyota are good-natured friends." I ask him why he wants to become a regular worker. "I like big companies," he answers. "They never go bankrupt." He dreams the same old dreams, stimulated by

56

the advertisement leaflets that come with our newspapers. He wants to rent an apartment, buy a washing machine, a color TV, a vacuum cleaner, etc. etc.

But Kudo's desires aren't unusual. Most of the young workers in the dormitory own color television sets, stereo radios, and cars. Their greatest desire, though, is to own their own houses. They usually get married soon after they complete the monthly payments for their electrical appliances and cars, but only a very few are lucky enough to live in company houses. Toyota doesn't even build them any more. Instead, it asks workers who have lived in the company houses for ten years to leave and advises them to buy their own houses. The majority of the workers in my workshop belong to a monthly home savings plan. After saving for one year under this plan, employees over twenty-five who have been with the company for over five years are entitled to a loan of $6,700 at 4.5 percent annual interest. The loan must be repaid in twelve years.

There is another system called a Toyota Loan. It is conducted with the cooperation of the Long-Term Credit Bank, and the maximum loan is $33,000 at an annual interest of 5.5 percent, payable in twenty-five years. Approximately 4,000 workers have supposedly bought houses built with the help of these two types of loans, and in a very real sense these young married men are tied to the company—that is, to the assembly line—by their loan payments until the day they retire.

Monday, October 16
During lunch break the team chief tells us that the line will run an extra hour in order to increase the output

to 760 boxes. Workers on both shifts are ordered to work together during that hour. We object loudly. The management did it once before when the line temporarily broke down and reduced output. They operated the line on a fifty-second cycle. We were forced to crowd together while we worked at top speed. It was really dangerous, and the electric tools hanging overhead sometimes hit us on the head.

"They're putting production before safety," someone says.

"That's suicide!"

"Not suicide," says one, laughing. "Murder."

"Damn! How can two shifts fit on one line?"

"If that impacter hits your head, you're going to see stars."

The team chief keeps silent through it all, but as soon as we start to work, he walks up and down along the line holding up a notice written on a piece of cardboard: "The line will be run for one hour with two shifts working together in order to produce 760 units." The noise in the workshop is so loud no one can hear him. It reminds me of the old feudal method of putting up government orders on posters. Probably because of the strong opposition, however, the line stops at 2:15, and we get together to have a meeting. The team chief and the foreman tell us that today the speed of the line has been increased and that we must "by all means" raise production even if we have to work overtime to meet the production target. One of the workers comments, "They used to put in enough workers to meet the target, but now all they care about is the amount of production."

There have been many accidents in this plant, and it has been put under surveillance. In order to "increase safety," it has been decided that for the next three months we must hold a ten-minute Safety First meeting every day before the line starts. However, the campaign has little more than a psychological effect. The "meeting" consists of chanting in chorus the safety slogan that the team chief reads to us. He sits facing us on a bench in the first row and drones on, "First of all, we must and must not do . . ." Then we repeat the slogan in unison. We feel embarrassed. Some say "And second . . ." as soon as the word "first" is repeated in unison. Some of the others mumble only the last phrase, or protest, "We aren't schoolboys." But somehow we all end up chanting the slogan in unison. The team chief continues reciting until he reaches the part that states, "Let's work with plenty of time and energy in reserve." He skips this part, saying, "That's impossible, since we're always pressed for time . . . aren't we?"

Since the canteen doesn't open until 5:30 A.M., workers living in the dormitory will be late for the meeting. The general foreman called the canteen and asked them to serve us earlier, but they refused. That means we have to eat our breakfast in an incredible hurry. So the speed of the "breakfast line" has also been increased.

After work, I take a small bus that runs between plants to the Takaoka plant. After a fifteen-minute walk to the Takaoka Fresh Breeze dorm, I meet Ishioka, a man from Hirosaki who was interviewed with me at the Public Employment Security Office and also came to work as a seasonal worker. Last night he called me up at my dorm to ask how I was. He's a farmer from an apple-orchard area twenty minutes' drive from my parents' farm. He owns a small rice

59

field and a small orchard. He worked for Honda as a seasonal worker until last year.

Ishioka answers the bell with a weary face. He's on the night shift and has only gotten up a few minutes earlier. Now he's doing his laundry. He and six other workers share three rooms. All of them are from farm areas. It's fall, and farmers all over the country are starting to go out and get winter jobs to tide them over until spring. Ishioka's work consists of three operations: tightening door bolts and trunk bolts and fixing small lamps for Corollas—all in fifty-eight seconds. Last night, he says, the dormitory loudspeaker was busy announcing telegrams from workers' families. Ishioka is a veteran seasonal worker and tells us, laughing, "Since the job is so tough, the guys ask their families to send telegrams asking them to come home, and they use them as excuses to quit."

Luckily, on my way home a gas station attendant offers me a ride. He mentions that a lot of Toyota workers quit during the midsummer and the New Year's vacations. The people from the area know how hard the job is, so they won't work for Toyota.

Tuesday, October 17
It's exactly a month today since I started working here.

I drop in on Kudo on my way home. He's pleased to see me and tries to say something, but I can't hear him at all over the noise. I watch for a while as he takes out two drive-shaft cylinders and screws them together at the center, then lifts the entire thing onto a tester. He makes the shaft turn, and if the weight of both sides is uneven, he balances them by welding on a metal tip. Then he marks it with a punch and applies grease and paint. For each operation, he has to lift and carry the heavy shaft. Finally, he lifts it to eye level and hangs it from a trolley conveyor. Moving in such a small space, with machines towering over him, always running, he works from eight in the morning until eight at night! It's amazing the human body can do it. No wonder he throws himself on his bed as soon as he comes back.

It's chilly. Winter's closing in.

Wednesday, October 18

Kudo wakes me up at six. I must have slept through my alarm clock—it's already light outside. I'm an hour late for work, but the team chief doesn't say anything about it. His expression seems to say, "I'm glad you came anyway." One worker's absence makes the burden heavier for all the others.

I got the receipt for the wages I'll get on the twentieth:

Wages

Basic pay with production allowance	$126.90
Overtime allowance (8.5 hours)	12.57
Overnight allowance (8.5 hours)	2.50
Shift allowance (8.5 hours)	12.57
Revision and supplement	1.66
Total	$156.20

Deductions

Health insurance premium	4.80
Social security	6.40
Unemployment insurance premium	1.01
Room	0.34
Total	$12.55
Net	$143.65

That night, I'd hardly gone to sleep when Miyamoto returned and woke me up with his ham radio. It was well past eleven when I finally got back to sleep. Early in the morning I woke up repeatedly, afraid that I might oversleep and be late for work again. It's horrible to work without enough sleep.

I had heard that people on the other shift worked overtime until one in the morning. The new work schedule was designed to squeeze up output and was to continue for a while yet. It's brutally simple. Management simply speeds up the conveyor belt, shortens the time given to each task, and ties the workers longer to the line.

Friday, October 20

Today is payday. I received $145. Printed on the envelope was Toyota's slogan "Good Ideas, Good Products." My actual pay is $143.65, but they rounded it off by lending me $1.35. It's painful to look at the money—only $145 for all that incredible work. My average gross pay per day is $11.17. If I were to work twenty-two days a month, my monthly salary would be between $243 and $250. A regular worker says to me, "I wish I was a seasonal worker." A seasonal worker's wage per day is higher than a regular worker's.

According to a worker, the ratio of basic pay to production allowance is 1:1.2, and the production allowance varies by $3.33 to $6.67 according to the monthly output of each workshop. The amount of output is calculated on the basis of the number of workers, the total working hours, and the number of boxes produced. When work is slack, they send workers off as "reinforcements" to other workshops. Seasonal workers and newcomers are also counted as full-fledged workers, so if these unskilled workers slow the line, it affects the production allowance, as does the quantity of factory supplies like oil and gloves. We all complain about the pay, yet it feels good to believe that our labor has some value. Even as we all gripe we all look pleased.

Saturday, October 21
Every day as I work I wait for many things:

- February 15 (the end of my contract: I'll be free, will get a $43.30 bonus, and will be entitled to unemployment insurance).
- the weekend (I'll rest).
- the end of work (I'll go back and sleep).
- the lunch break (the line will stop and I'll sit and rest and smoke).

Only in this way can I force myself to go on from second to second and minute to minute, to make time pass.

The *Asahi Daily* has an interesting article by a correspondent in the United States entitled "Modern Times Modernized." The Lordstown General Motors plant has been the site of a number of acts of sabotage in the last few months. Angered by the inhumane working conditions, workers have simply walked out of their workshops, leaving the moving line behind. Engine parts arrived unassembled at the end of the line. Windows of finished cars were broken, seats were slashed with knives, dashboards were smashed with hammers. Every time one of these "accidents" happened, the line was stopped and the defective cars were sent to the repair section. Operation efficiency dropped by half.

The workers were rebelling. But the most amazing part of the article is that the correspondent reported that he saw workers smoking and chatting while they worked on the line. Those with free time gathered at a table in the corner and played cards. Dissatisfaction among workers grew very strong when the production schedule was raised from 60 to 100 cars per hour, and the workers reacted with sabotage. How could they smoke and play cards when the speed of the line was increased to raise productivity? The article says that the time allowed for one operation was reduced to thirty-six seconds, but that only ten seconds were actually needed. GM workers are well treated as compared with Toyota workers. It's hard to believe.

Wednesday, October 25
Worked for an hour and a half after supper and felt so tired and worn out that I thought many times of stopping and going back to my room. But strangely enough, I kept on repeating my operations and endured until the line stopped.

During supper the foreman distributed a form asking us to support Takezo Watanabe, a candidate from the Democratic Socialist Party. The company and the union have joined to back Watanabe, and posters supporting Watanabe are on the company bulletin boards. The foreman also asked us to write down the names of our relatives on the form. "What's the use of supporting that guy?" someone protested. "It won't raise our wages. Watanabe's from the Mechanical Department of the Head Office, and he knows the working conditions in our transmission workshop. But what has he done for us?" Still, I suspect most of the workers will vote for Watanabe come election day.

Thursday, October 26

Overtime until midnight. After work the team chief spends twenty minutes explaining how to read an "interlighter," an iron flag carrying manufacturing information. Different car models and parts are designated by different symbols and numbers according to which they are shipped to the final assembly shop or to the Toyota Auto Body Company. I can recognize only four kinds on the list. There are at least ten types of car transmissions, ninety if classified in detail. This is all new to me. "I never knew this type existed," one worker says. "I don't understand this at all," another says. "Those English letters, they're a secret code." Until now we've only been taught our own individual operations, and we don't know anything about what others are doing. Our jobs would be a lot easier if we only knew a few things about how they fit into the whole picture. One of the workers demanded a chance to broaden his knowledge, so the management held today's lecture. But this is so formal and dry that we just stand here, staring at the team chief.

I'm getting to know my co-workers fairly well.

Shimoyama is twenty-three and graduated from a commercial high school in Miyagi Prefecture five years ago. He wanted to be a policeman, but he couldn't get a job. He worked at a couple of other Toyota plants before coming to this workshop. At each plant, he found the working conditions worse than at the plant before. He's the most outspoken in my group and often lights the alarm light to call the team chief. He also takes his time going to the toilet or having a smoke. But he's a brisk worker, sometimes even smiling. His hobbies are driving and mah-jongg. He lives in a small apartment near the plant and comes to work by car. Has a one-year-old baby girl.

Iino is nineteen and stands at the end of our line. He comes from Hananomaki in Iwate Prefecture. After he dropped out of a fishery high school, he tried working in Tokyo and then came to Toyota. Shortly after he got here two years ago, he had intestinal trouble and was hospitalized at the Toyota Hospital, where he lost twenty-two pounds. He became a regular worker last year and plans to marry in a year or two. If he does, he'll never be able to quit the job. He often goes bowling and lives in the bachelors' dormitory next to mine.

Murayama, at twenty-seven the subchief, graduated from high school in Oita Prefecture in Kyushu eight years ago. He's the most productive worker in our group and is very popular. He's the only one in the group who wears glasses. He's modest and often says, "This job's good enough for me, a guy without brains." His wife is expecting a baby soon. He likes mah-jongg and bowling. He lives in a company house next to my dorm and comes to work by car.

Sugimoto is twenty-two and graduated from high school in Okazaki four years ago. He's always dressed in neat white overalls. He loves to read newspapers and sometimes talks about what he reads. He likes dancing and skiing. His right index finger has a scar. Maybe from an injury he got on the job? He comes to work by car from Okazaki.

Fukuyama is forty. He's one of the reinforcement group from the chassis workshop. Sometimes he falls behind the pace of the line, but when he's working well, he rushes through his operation, lights a cigarette, and smokes as he works. He has the toughest work on the line: holding up a welded gear box with one hand and placing it on the conveyor. Reinforcements and seasonal workers are usually assigned the hardest jobs. He often says, "This is tough. I didn't come all the way to Toyota to do a job like this! I'm a welder with a national license!" Before he came here, he worked at a chemical plant in Omuta in Kyushu. He enjoys cultivating miniature trees.

Harada is twenty-five and graduated from high school in Hiroshima Prefecture. He also works briskly. He's a good-looking guy who comes to work in his suit and tie. He usually leaves right at finishing time. They say he's a devoted husband. He's been working at Toyota for seven years. He lives in a small apartment near the plant.

Yoshizaki is twenty-seven and comes from Kagoshima Prefecture in Kyushu. He's been at Toyota for six years. Before that, he served in the Self-Defense Forces. He's a quiet, sober man. He lives in a company house with his wife and two sons and comes to work by car. He loves driving and drinking.

Sugiura (twenty-six or twenty-seven) is from Hokkaido. Also from the Self-Defense Forces, he now has a heavy beard and a hot temper. When he argues with the team chief he uses very strong language.

Mikami is twenty-six or seven and is also from Hokkaido. He's a heavy drinker like Yoshizaki, though very quiet.

Takeda is nineteen and comes from Shizuoka Prefecture. A graduate of Toyota Vocational High School, he's quiet on the job, but we always go home together. He's in the mountain-climbing club and goes climbing every Sunday. He lives in a small apartment near my dorm. He pays $17 a month for a room of four-and-a-half tatami mats.*

Ashino is only eighteen. He's a seasonal worker from Asahikawa, Hokkaido. In his home town, he worked as an assistant to a truck driver while attending commercial high school at night. He came here after reading a Toyota ad in the newspapers: "Light, simple job." He often complains, "They lied straight-faced. The job's heavy and complicated." He can't sleep well at night because of pains in his legs.

The team chief is thirty and comes from Miyazaki Prefecture in Kyushu. He's been in the factory for eight years and speaks Nagoya dialect well. He always looks pale. He owns a house near the plant. He likes mahjongg and bowling.

Friday, October 27

Two new seasonal workers arrive. Both are around twenty and from Hokkaido. One's a carpenter and the other a farmer. The farmer is very interested in parts.

---

* About 8½ square yards.

He toys with them and asks eagerly, "How much over-time can we do?" He seems full of confidence. The carpenter looks depressed.

Kudo told me that his team chief told him to stay away from a certain worker with whom he had started to make friends. Once the fellow brought his girlfriend to the dorm and was deprived of overtime work for breaking regulations. That's hard to understand. It's unreasonable, to say the least, that our privacy should be controlled by the management. Kudo told me the fellow had to leave the dorm and rent an apartment (which costs him $20 a month), as well as buy some furniture. He also has to pay the monthly installments on his car. Kudo is sorry for him because without the overtime allowances he'll be hard up.

Sunday, October 29

I go for a walk with Kudo. There are lots of fields around the dormitory where tea plants are cultivated. The farmers' houses are big and look comfortable. The area is called Hoei-Cho (Toyota Prosperity Town), after Sakichi Toyoda, the founder of the company. (*Ho* is the same Chinese character as *Toyo* in Toyoda, or Toyota, *ei* means "to prosper," and *cho* means "dis-trict.") The address of the Head Office is 1 Toyota-Cho, the very center of Toyota City. Hoei-Cho is the surrounding area.

Monday, October 30

Around six, as I'm about to leave the dining room after supper, I run into Ashino, one of the new workers from Hokkaido. He's well built, with hair down to his shoulders. He stands there with his shoulders hunched as if he's been waiting for something. I picked him out early among all the young regular workers. I often think when I look around at the people in the canteen that even when they're not in their uniforms, but all wearing what they want to wear, they all look very much alike. Maybe it's because they're all young and unmarried that they give off the same passive feeling a bunch of students cramming for college entrance examinations. They're so quiet and look so beaten. Hardly a single one exhibits a striking personality or even a defiant look. If there is anyone who stands out from the crowd it's usually a seasonal worker. They at least have their own unique experiences and life histories. They have an individual air about them, and it is this difference that makes Ashino stand out in the crowd. He didn't come to the workshop today and looked refreshed after a good day's rest.

"Hi, Ashino, the work bother you?" He pauses a few moments before replying.

"I'm going to quit. Got a new job. I went to Nagoya yesterday and saw an ad in a pinball parlor. They offered me $133 a month. Take-home pay, that is."

"You look relieved."

"Yes, in a way I am," he says. "It's a relief to think I don't have to go back to that stinking plant. Still, I envy people who can stick at their jobs. I'm embarrassed to quit now. I just wrote to my family and friends that I'd try my luck at Toyota. But I can't sleep at night thinking about my jobs. First I do one thing, then another, then something even more boring—on and on. Damn, the company should treat us better." He pauses, then continues, "Want to know something? My roommate says that five hundred workers a month quit. I'd rather dig ditches than work here. And that bastard section manager, he really pisses me off. In the beginning he told me he'd change my position and asked me to hang on, but in the end he said, 'Well, maybe it's best if you do leave.' What kind of a game does he think he's playing? But still"—he's putting a brave face on it—"maybe it *is* best to have a job where you can wear a suit and tie." Poor kid. Though Ashino's strong and healthy, he couldn't stand the job for more than one week. The probationer who arrived with him also disappeared after only one day.

Later, Kudo returns to the room furious: "The company sure cares a lot more about production than it does about our health." He says the daily output of the drive shafts has been increased from 600 to 700. The workers, though, have to fill the new quota in exactly the same time—from eight in the morning to seven at night. Last year his job was done by three workers, but now he's left to do the entire job alone. Also, two members of the work group have been absent for several days. In spite of this, the company imposes this new quota of a hundred more drive shafts. At a meeting during lunch break, Kudo's general foreman made a speech on the new quota and concluded sternly, "Just don't make mistakes."

The company always fills up the work breaks with speeches and orders. Once in my workshop, the general foreman spent ten minutes encouraging us to submit "Good Idea Suggestions." He left thirty blank sheets with the foreman to be filled with the "good ideas." That's two sheets for each worker in the group. The number of "Good Idea Suggestions" submitted by the workers are posted on a large sheet of paper on the locker-room wall. Insurance companies post the same type of business records for their individual salesmen. Records, records, records.

Tuesday, October 31

October is finally over. My third month begins tomorrow. It's hard to believe. The mornings and evenings are chilly now, and I see more middle-aged men at the canteen and the plant—all new seasonal workers, most of them farmers from the country.

The individual numbers printed on the time cards for new seasonal workers are all above 900. My number is 639. In other words, nearly 300 workers have arrived after me. The *Toyota* reported in its October 13 issue that 150 have joined since August. That makes some 400 new workers altogether. There are frequent want-ads in the newspapers, and many more workers will be coming.

My head is still ringing from being hit by Takeda's impactor (a hand-held, powered screwdriver) a few days ago. It's not unusual: almost all the workers on the assembly line have been hit once or twice by these hard-to-control tools. "Seeing stars in the daytime" is a Toyota tradition.

3

D R O P O U T S

Wednesday, November 1

I'm not myself while I'm on the line. So busy that I'm always carried with the transmissions along the line, it often surprises me to look up and suddenly find some strange scene in front of my eyes. In that split second I always wonder where I am. Merely seeing the light come in through a door on the opposite side of the building can bowl me over. So intently have I been watching the minute world filled with auto parts that when I look up it's as if I've landed in another world. Sometimes when I'm working, I suddenly realize that my hands are deftly assembling with no signal from my mind. Again, for a few seconds, I'm totally disoriented. Then my consciousness catches up with my hands' motions and I come back to myself—"Yeah, I'm doing all right." My hands have kept moving by a conditioned reflex. I keep remembering Chaplin.

I know I should always keep in mind that I'm making transmissions, important car parts, but I simply can't imagine that this box will become part of a car carrying people, a car that will move through a world full of people. I simply move my hands so that each box will move down the line before the next one arrives.

The company has posted a notice on the company bulletin board:

WE ACHIEVED A PRODUCTION LEVEL
OF 210,000 CARS A MONTH TODAY.
THANK YOU FOR YOUR COOPERATION.
THE PRESIDENT

Toyota is the first Japanese auto company to turn out 200,000 cars in a single month.

There's some new graffiti on the toilet wall in the dorm. One goes:

Toyotapeople aren't people, only machines.

I don't suppose the guy who wrote that is still here at Toyota.

Thursday, November 2

Another notice on the board today—this time a list of the number of senior employees to be given recognition for long service:

—LENGTH OF SERVICE	NUMBER OF WORKERS—
35 YEARS	99
30 YEARS	132
25 YEARS	221
20 YEARS	0
15 YEARS	99

These figures are small in proportion to the total number of 40,000 workers.

Friday, November 3

It's the anniversary of the founding of the company, a holiday.

"Kosuke Gomi Protests," which has been serialized in the *Shincho Weekly,* ended this week. It was a curious article. You'd expect that the name of Gomi, a very famous writer, would appear in the table of contents, but it was not even mentioned. The article (twenty-three pages in all) was submitted "Sponsored by Toyota Motor Company." Though it had the appearance of a report, Toyota actually paid Gomi to write it. According to Gomi, Toyota engineers have been exhausting themselves doing research on emission-control devices. His "protest" was not on behalf of those who suffer from exhaust pollution but, rather, represented the protest of automakers against the Tokyo prefectural government's attempt to regulate gas emissions. After listing Toyota engineers' arguments against the prefectural governor, Gomi tactfully inserted his own opinion: "All the citizens of the nation are responsible for pollution"—the old tactic of blaming both parties equally, which results in nobody being wrong. He continued suavely: "The whole population of Tokyo is responsible for air pollution, that much we must admit. The government should not be accused, but neither should we blame the auto manufacturers. Let me repeat: everyone living in the city is responsible."

Even as the article appeared, the Environmental Protection Agency had released findings that made it very clear that the principal air-pollution offenders were automobiles. Gomi quickly snapped at the newspaper reporters who had published the findings and ordered them not to go by car to gather news. Meanwhile, he wrote only of Toyota's "safety measures." The last installment was headlined: "To our friends at Toyota, the number one automaker." Ah, Gomi, you pathetic cheerleader. What a bumbling old samurai you've become!

Sunday, November 5

The third and the fourth of this month were company holidays. Though today is Sunday, we're on duty. One of the first things you learn is that the Toyota calendar is different from the one "out there." Toyota workers say "out there" in the same way that prisoners talk of "the outside." For example, "You'd better go to a doctor out there instead of the Toyota Hospital."

Tuesday, November 7

On the line, time passes slowly because we work counting every minute and second. Last night we stayed late, until twelve-forty, which meant an hour and forty minutes overtime on the line. After that, Fukuyama and I sat on parts boxes facing each other and fitted the rubbers on the speedometer shafts until one-thirty. "Wish all overtime work were easy like this," I said, laughing. "The labor productivity at Toyota," he joked, "is as good as that in the United States—and the pay is as low as that of Japan."

During supper break, I hear a seasonal worker from Tokushima saying to another young seasonal worker, "I guess I'll quit." Later I walk to the canteen with a forty-four-year-old seasonal worker from Kumamoto, who tells me his contract will expire next April. He's surprised at the intensity of the work here and says, "I can see how they make these big profits." He once worked at Kawasaki Steel, and tells me that things there were much more relaxed.

The union is advertising the fact that it's negotiating a business-trip allowance. I am mad. How many of us on the line will ever make a business trip?

78

Wednesday, November 8

It's past time to report, but I'm still in bed. I'll be an hour late today.

Yesterday the line stopped for an hour during the other shift because of machine trouble, and it ran two hours extra on our shift. After that, it took us thirty minutes more to fit the rubbers onto the speedometer shafts—until one-thirty. A few of us dropped into a bar on the way home for some *sake* and noodles. I drank with Kon, who's about twenty and from Asahikawa. "It's amazing," he said, "how the regulars can bear the situation." It was three before I got home.

The forty-four-year-old seasonal worker didn't show up. He was already worn out on the second day. That makes two out of six seasonal workers on our shift who have now quit, plus one probationer. Two seasonal workers on the other shift have also quit.

Kon was hired with eighty-seven others—the groups are getting bigger. I see want-ads in the *Chunichi Daily* two or three times a week now. When I was hired, the year-end allowance was $17. Now it's been doubled. According to Kudo, the company managed to recruit only half the workers it wanted this year.

During the break, everybody sits on the bench, exhausted.

"Do you think they'll take responsibility if my wife runs away?" twenty-three-year-old Shimoyama says, not quite joking. "I haven't screwed her for a long time."

"Yeah, I can't get it up either," someone else says.

"So what? You're a bachelor."

"It matters, man, it matters."

79

"I used to be as hard as that steel pole over there, but now, I envy my little finger."

Everyone laughs.

"I didn't see a single car on the way home last night," said Sugimoto, who drives his own car to work.

"Not last night, this morning."

More laughs.

"They should build company housing around the plant so we could sleep a little."

"Hell, then we'd be living in the plant."

"Then let me come to your wife's. I'll take care of her."

By now everyone is listening and commenting. "Last night I fell asleep in the bathtub and my wife woke me up," Fukuyama says. Murayama has also been home late every night. He takes his glasses off, blinks his eyes, and says, "My sight's getting a lot worse."

"If someone died on the line, would they realize how bad it's getting?"

"One wouldn't be enough."

"How about everybody on the line?"

"The other shift would have to die, too."

"Still not enough."

Somehow, complaints about bad working conditions always turn into jokes. Nobody listens to our complaints, so it's easier to joke.

Friday, November 10

Kon, a seasonal worker, finally quit. I'll never forget how he used to get angry and say "Bullshit." He filled in the questionnaire that those who quit are supposed to answer. Someone found it on the general foreman's desk. Under "Impressions" he had scribbled, "The pay's terrible considering how hard the work is!" We were all excited and passed it around. The others asked me to "fill out the form truthfully when you quit, too."

"If we speak out now," one of the regulars said, "we'll suffer for at least ten years."

"How about the union? Won't they take care of you?" I asked.

"The union works for the management," one of them replied, and shrugged his shoulders.

With Kon gone, there are only three seasonal workers left out of our six. Two regulars in Kudo's team quit. One of the regular workers said to me, "Only screwballs or idiots would stay with this job." He sounded as if he hated himself.

I get a card from Ishioka, who has left the Takaoka plant and returned to his home town. He writes:

Just wanted to drop you a line. I came home because my arms are in bad shape. I'll let you know when I come back so we can get together. Please take care of yourself. This morning we had our first snow.

I remember how pale his face was when I saw him in the dorm the other day.

All letters are delivered to the dorm office first. The supervisor then sticks them according to room number into a small pigeonhole cabinet at the corner of the dining room. I strongly suspect he reads them.

Saturday, November 11

We on the second shift get the day off today. I stay in bed all day long. Thick black curtains hang down and completely cover the dorm windows. We see many of these curtains drawn during the day. The shift changes from night to day once a week. Someone remarked that we're like hens being "protected" so we can lay eggs for the company.

Monday, November 13

I'm on the first shift today. We work two hours overtime—I'm exhausted. I had a terrible toothache last night, but I got hold of a painkiller.

I came back with Kinoshita, who's about fifty and from Sado. This is his third year at Toyota as a seasonal worker. His number is 8819170, which means that he's the 531st seasonal worker after me. Now that he's here, the line has ten regular workers (two of them are reinforcements), four seasonal workers, and one probationer.

Tuesday, November 14

Our conversation at lunchtime is about Iino's wedding, set for next year. He and the girl are from the same home town, but they met in Tokyo. Toyota workers tend to get married fairly young—Iino's not yet twenty —and I wonder if it has anything to do with the monotony of the work.

"You'll have to work harder," someone teases.

"Damn, how can I work harder?" Iino counters, and we all laugh.

Even Kudo, who once dreamed of being a regular, now talks about going home at the end of December. Two full months have passed since our arrival. By now, I'm used to the work, but it doesn't get any easier physically. The exhaustion just seems to accumulate.

The line now turns out 46 boxes an hour. If everything goes well, 345 boxes are produced between 6:00 A.M. and 2:15 P.M., and 770 by midnight if the night shift does an hour of overtime.

Wednesday, November 15

As soon as I return to my room, I stick my feet by the heater and fall asleep. I can't stay awake. I could hardly eat my supper because of my toothache. I'll go to the dentist as soon as I'm paid.

I had diarrhea today and had to go to the toilet twice while I was on the line. It must have been the painkiller, combined with the terrible canteen food, sheer exhaustion, and the mental pressure of following the line. Still, I hated to light the lamp and call the team chief. Even though it feels wonderful to leave the line just for five minutes, I feel strangely guilty when I do.

I talked for a while at changing time with a probationer on the other shift. He told me that during his six months of probation, he gets paid monthly on a daily-pay basis. It works out to $20 less than what the regular workers get. The probationers consider themselves lucky if they become regular workers after six months. Should they miss a day or two of work, the promotion could take a year, and many of them quit before the year is up. So, in the end, the company makes a good profit: the probationers work harder for less pay, and then quit, disgusted.

I got my pay slip: "One day's absence, twenty-two days' work." My basic pay is $200.60; the overtime allowance, $31.10; the night allowance, $5.80; and the shift allowance, $25.10. From the total $262.60, I take home $247, and from that, they've subtracted the $23 I borrowed in advance to buy the meal tickets, leaving me only $224. But the young regular workers are envious of seasonal workers, who get more than they do. Kudo told me his team chief said to him, "You're here to make money, aren't you? Why don't you work harder?" They act as though "seasonal worker" means "money grubber." Actually, most seasonal workers are farmers who leave their homes during the off season to try to make ends meet. Sixteen or seventeen years ago, when I graduated from high school and worked in a small factory in Tokyo, the men there found out I was from the north and asked me cuttingly if I was a seasonal worker. Little has changed over the years. When I stayed in some housing for workers in north Kyushu only two years ago, the other workers found out that I was from the north. Their only comment was "So you're one of those seasonal workers." Even among the workers the expression is used with contempt.

The *Toyota Weekly* reports that the union won the full bonus it demanded—3.1 months' pay, an average of $718. But since this amount was already stipulated in last summer's agreement on the annual bonus, they hardly "won everything we demanded." Besides, only a part of it will be paid in cash on December 1. Out of $718, $633 is calculated according to the worker's basic pay, which is $113 for a worker 28.2 years of age, with 5.9 years of service and 1.1 dependents. That's really cheap! Of the remaining $85, $27 is the service allowance, which is determined by the requirements of the job, and $58 is the performance allowance, which is determined by the abilities of the worker. The probationer will get an amount equal to 76 days' pay.

Friday, November 17

The week's finally over, and I'm gaining confidence that somehow I'll last until February 15, when my contract expires.

I nearly died of toothache after lunch—had to take more painkiller. It was hard to move on the line.

A seasonal worker, eighteen and from Hidaka in Hokkaido, came in on the other shift. Before Toyota, he had worked as a carpenter. A lot of carpenters, seasonal workers from Hokkaido, were leaving their families behind. He himself was replacing a seasonal worker who had quit. Word spread along the line that he and his three roommates had lost all their money when someone broke into their dorm room. There were no suspects.

In the evening, Kudo and I talk for a while. I ask him if he knows that Honda is giving workers free meals. "Kamata," he says, "I didn't know you read newspaper ads, too!"

Saturday, November 18

It's the third Saturday and a holiday. My toothache's getting even worse.

This morning, Kudo is getting ready to go on a day trip to Gamagori with the guys on his team, humming as he polishes his shoes, then putting on a blue shirt and a light jacket. But suddenly, he lies down with a headache and nosebleed.

"It's because of that accident," he says. The trip is canceled.

I get a call from Ishioka. We chat for a while, and he says he's been working at the Honda Suzuka plant. We agree to meet tomorrow in Nagoya.

Sunday, November 19

Today, I met Ishioka at Nagoya station. He worked at Toyota for eleven days, though he wanted to quit sooner. All employees must work eleven days to qualify for unemployment insurance. When he gave his notice, the team chief tried to persuade him to stay, even if only for one more day. He even confessed he himself wanted to quit. Ishioka is now working as a welder for Honda. It isn't easy work, but by and large, he says, the job is better. He's not as pressed as he used to be at Toyota, and the meals are free, even with a bottle of milk. We meet at a restaurant, but my toothache returns, and I can't eat.

The November 17 issue of the *Toyota* headlined "Brilliant Record Achieved." In this, its thirty-fourth year, Toyota's total production output has reached 10 million—a new record in the history of the auto industry of Japan. In February 1969, the production output reached 5 million. In the next three years, it doubled. By October 1972 output exceeded 200,000 a month. Now it's approaching the target of 2,100,000 a year. A second assembly line in the Takaoka plant has begun full operation, and this, together with the policy of full-capacity operation in all Toyota plants through the introduction of the "intensive reinforcement system" and extra working hours on holidays, accounted for the record. The article continued excitedly:

> In order to shake off the desperate pursuit of other auto companies and to catch up with the two biggest companies in the world, each one of us must always try to surpass the others in every single section of the company. Toyota demands that every worker con-

stantly offer all his abilities and exert himself to promote productivity. We must always try to improve ourselves so we can contribute more and function better.

The article did not ask at what price to the workers Toyota runs this desperate race.

Astoundingly, this simple, repetitive, unskilled labor makes it difficult for workers to quit. Some, like Takeda, a young probationer, seem serious about quitting. He'd like to work in a mountain-climbing equipment store. But even if he were lucky enough to get that kind of job, it wouldn't give him the $200 a month he earns at Toyota.

Others in his club are very depressed and frustrated on the job, too. Most of them are unsuccessful in climbing the company ladder, and in a way mountain climbing keeps them going—though some of them still dream of becoming a team chief.

Most of these workers are still single. When you reach a certain age and get a certain wage, you can no longer afford to leave the company. No matter how boring the work is, you'd get less somewhere else. Eventually, young workers full of potential are deadened by the monotonous, unchallenging work. Slowly but surely, they enter a permanently closed society. "Rationalization" of production changes even their personalities by making them overstrain a tiny fraction of their abilities. Ultimately, it's a kind of lobotomy.

I wonder if the line work actually is "unskilled labor." By the time one new worker has "settled down," many others have quit. It took me a full month to get used to the speed of the line. Only three people, the foreman, the team chief, and the subchief, are able to handle each process of the transmission assembly. But in reality, they're neither unskilled nor skilled—not even half-skilled. Their jobs have nothing at all to do with skill. Like the rest of us—the so-called "single-skill workers"—they go through motions that are not "skills" in any sense of the word, just primitive movements. It's said that Sakichi Toyoda tried to invent a perpetual-motion machine using human beings.

The *Toyota Weekly* ran an article entitled "Shop Meetings Demand the Five-Day Week." We work overtime every day, even on Saturdays. What kind of five-day week are they trying to introduce?

Sunday, November 26
I take off three days. The twenty-fifth and twenty-sixth were holidays, and I went up to Tokyo to have my teeth treated.

Monday, November 27
One thing you notice rather quickly is that anyone who comes here with any experience soon leaves. One probationer quit so quickly that all I learned about him was that he once repaired telephone-exchange machines. He wanted to become a Toyota regular but gave up the idea. Sometimes I wonder if those who quit are normal and human, while we who remain are the abnormal ones. Those who stay seem to lack self-respect. If you want to think and act independently, you can't stay.

Those of us who remain have to find some pleasure somehow. Shimoyama, for instance, works ahead and then comes to help me. He takes over my position, puts the six bolts into the lock, and tightens them all at once with a nut runner—which takes some skill. When he succeeds he yells excitedly. I do too, whenever I can manage it. Completing the task in two or three seconds, hearing the bolts slide in with a nice click, gives me real pleasure. Even in this kind of detailed, boring work, you need some sort of satisfaction, or you can't go on.

While I was away, the probationer quit and Takeda was off climbing Mount Fuji. Minus three workers, the others had to work overtime until past two every night. When I returned, neither the foreman nor the team chief was angry. The general foreman only said, "Don't stay away any more, OK?" and patted me on the shoulder. The first day of work I missed, the fore-man had also taken the day off, so the general foreman phoned him and ordered him to come. Kudo told me a man from the personnel section came looking for me. "He was mad," Kudo said—even though I'd phoned the personnel office to tell them I was taking the day off. The man who answered the phone was careful to ask if I was coming the next day. Takeda had to file a "permission for absence" form three weeks in advance before he could take a day off. We don't even have the freedom to rest.

A worker was killed in an accident at the Kamigo Toyota plant, though it wasn't reported in the news-papers.

Tuesday, November 28

Overslept again. Thirty minutes late. I still get very tired, even after almost three months. "It's only natu-ral," Fukuyama says. "We're running a race against stopwatches and computers." During the break Yoshi-zaki, who is sitting next to me, says, "Whenever I work on the second shift, I can only sleep five hours. On Saturdays, all of a sudden I collapse."

Wednesday, November 29
Since a farewell "party" is planned at noon for a worker who retires today, the line doesn't stop once between six and twelve. At noon, people gather in a half-circle in front of the canteen. A middle-aged man with glasses stands in the center, and his boss beside him makes a speech, using a portable microphone. Forced to attend this meeting, we have no lunch break. The canteen is packed and full of noise. People are jamming in, pushing the others.

On the general foreman's desk is an autograph album dedicated to Takezo Watanabe's candidacy for the House of Representatives. Watanabe is a candidate of the Democratic Socialist Party. The general foreman was asking each worker who came in to punch his time card to sign it. That's hard to refuse.

Thursday, November 30
The whole plant is closed for inventory. I slept from ten last night until late this afternoon.

In the evening, I went out to a bar. There, a group of workers around an oil heater were discussing just what caused the death of a worker in the Kamigo plant. The accident happened during lunch break. The worker was repairing a machine (naturally, he had to do it on his lunch time!). He got caught between a beam for replacing parts, and the machine. There was no one near by to hear his calls, and he died unnoticed. He was dead for an hour before they discovered his body.

Today's *Chunichi Daily* reports that Honda has

90

agreed to let Toyota use its CVCC motor in Toyota cars. Toyota first planned to use a rotary engine developed by Toyo Kogyo (Mazda). This engine has a fairly good emission-control device, but evidently it was expensive, since Toyota switched to the Honda engine, which barely meets the emission control law standards. In the past Toyota has preferred to spend money on expanding "rationalized" production and marketing rather than on developing an adequate engine.

4

MORE PRODUCTION MORE ACCIDENTS MORE DISSATISFACTION

Friday, December 1

Finally, it's December. On my way back, snow and sleet. Today is also year-end bonus day, and we huddle together on our benches and read the bonus pay slip. Actually only half the bonus was paid today. It's company policy to hold the remainder until the end of the year. Their idea seems to be to collect interest, and also, they hope to keep workers from quitting during the month. And by delaying full payment, Toyota can assert its arbitrary power over us while still making us feel "grateful" for what is our due. They pay each seasonal worker $33, but they take their time about it.

Saturday, December 2

Another cold day. The door at the end of the line opens to let in fork-lifts, and the cold wind blows in. Our teeth rattle louder than the assembly line. The plant's hot in the summer and cold in the winter. It certainly wasn't built with our health in mind.

Miura (who's twenty and a seasonal worker from Tokushima) and I go to see the truck assembly plant on our way back. Miura graduated from high school and took college entrance exams, but he failed the exams and worked at a printing factory for a while.

Beside the line in the assembly plant, there are fork-lifts and trucks—the latter loaded with tires, driver's seats, and assembled chassis parts—moving through the building. It's dangerous just walking through the traffic. Chassises come in and are put on the line near the entrance. First the axles are attached to the engines, and then the transmissions that we assembled are put in. The chassises look like giant queen bees followed by young workers.

The most telling aspect of the conveyor work is the tire installation. The work consists of putting on three tires every minute and forty seconds. The worker catches a tire that comes rolling down the ramp behind him, which he then rolls to the chassis. Pressing a pedal, he lifts the tire and puts it on the axle. Then he inserts six bolts and tightens them with a big nut runner. By then, the rear axle has arrived in front of him. He then rolls two tires joined together to the chassis, installs them, and inserts the bolts. He tightens these bolts with a big nut runner that he braces on his hipbone. As the bolts spin tight, another chassis arrives. He goes to get another tire . . .

Today's paper reports that the president of Toyota announced at a press conference that next year's production output target is 2,350,000 cars—a 15 percent increase for domestic cars and a 13 percent increase for exports.

Sunday, December 3
Yamamoto—who joined Toyota with me and lives on the same floor—comes to use our washing machine. He tells us that there was talk in his shop about the worker killed at the Kamigo plant. His wife was pregnant. In front of the coffin, there had been a new cap with a yellow line showing that the dead man had been promoted to team chief, plus a letter of promo-

tion. He was thirty and a subchief, and had been given a special promotion. Yamamoto said, "He didn't die in battle like a soldier. What is the management thinking?"

The notice on the company bulletin board doesn't mention the death. There is nothing but a message from the president: "I am sorry to inform you that a serious accident has occurred." Obviously, they don't feel much responsibility for the killing. On the same bulletin board, there is a notice from the union (at Toyota, the union doesn't have its own bulletin board and uses a corner of the company's board):

WE PRAY FOR THE PEACEFUL REPOSE OF TAKESHI NAKAI (THIRTY YEARS OLD), WHO DIED IN AN OCCUPATIONAL ACCIDENT AT THE NUMBER 55 MACHINERY SECTION, NUMBER 3 MACHINERY DEPARTMENT, KAMIGO PLANT, ON NOVEMBER 25 AT 12:10. SINCERE CONDOLENCES.

Condolences are one thing, but not a word of protest against the company! Both the company and the union seem to blame the accident on the carelessness of the victim.

Yamamoto tells us of another accident at his plant. A drill bit broke off and ripped into the neck of a worker who was standing near by. Most of the machines at the main plant date back to 1938 and are worn out. It's no surprise that accidents are becoming more and more frequent.

Thursday, December 7
When I get to the line, I notice an oil feeder with a thin plastic hose hanging overhead. The team chief

tells me to oil the gears when an RK or RY transmission comes by. Another operation! Already, there's barely enough time to do the regular job. As it is, the inspector puts in oil anyway. So I won't unless the team chief comes around. This must be one of the "Good Idea Suggestions" some worker made in order to fulfill his assignment.

Overtime again tonight. Today's total output is 785 boxes: 345 by the first shift and 440 by the second shift. Production is steadily increasing.

When I return to my room, Kudo's still in bed. He's late for work. Some machinery had broken down, and he had to work from eight last night until nine this morning. "By the time I got back," he says, "they'd stopped serving breakfast." He eats some bread and canned fish he has bought instead, and goes back to bed, saying he'll sleep until seven.

Friday, December 8

About nine in the evening, I ask the foreman, when he passes by, how long we have to work. "Only until twelve," he says. "There isn't much left." Right after the foreman leaves, I tell Fukuyama, on my right, that we'll finish by twelve, but he doesn't seem to believe me. Then I tell Takeda, on my left, who only says, "Is that so?" and doesn't seem to believe me either. Everybody is convinced they'll have to work until one o'clock. Or are they simply pretending they have to work late, so they can enjoy it when the work stops earlier? The line stops at twelve, but they still don't believe it—sometimes the management stops the line for five or six seconds to let a slow worker catch up. When the guys see that the electricity has gone off completely and that the end-of-work signal has been given, they cheer and clap. Everyone has been waiting for this moment.

My wrist aches so much I can hardly write this. I hope it won't become an "occupational disease."

Saturday, December 9

Toyota's production for November was 193,034 cars, which was a 4.5 percent increase from the previous November and the second highest monthly production in Toyota history. This figure included 51,793 small trucks, an increase of 7.5 percent over the previous year. No wonder we're so busy.

One night this week, the loudspeaker began paging "Mr. X of Room X. A phone call from Hirosaki." He was a new seasonal worker, and remembering a trip I once made in his region, I suddenly wanted to meet him and talk with him. I was traveling by train and I was sitting across from two farmers' wives in their forties. They were complaining loudly: one of their husbands had spent all the money he earned as a seasonal worker at a cabaret. Coming home, he had apologized and promised he'd never do it again. "Men are all like that," his wife said, "but what good did it do the children, who suffered most? How can he ever make up the loss of not being with his growing children?"

In a booklet that I got from the West County Teachers' Union in Aomori Prefecture, there was a paragraph about the mothers who work as seasonal workers and are forced to leave their children at home:

"Why don't you read the letter from your daughter? Three of us just read ours, and we laughed and cried, didn't we?" But still Mrs. Kase wouldn't open the letter her daughter Junko asked me to give to her. "No, I'll read it tonight, all by myself. I know I'll cry," she said, with tears in her eyes. She could never finish reading her daughter's letters at one time. She always read them bit by bit . . . in the evening . . . crying. Mrs. Kase only read a file of children's compositions, which their teacher had asked me to bring, but she didn't open Junko's letter while we were there.*

When I visited this mother, who worked together with her husband as a seasonal worker, she was getting ready to leave home for another season of migrant labor. She talked only a little with me, and soon her eyes were filled with tears.

After work, I call home. My wife's worried that she might have a premature birth.

Sunday, December 10

At eight o'clock there is an announcement over the dorm loudspeaker: "Please remember that today is election day for the House of Representatives." Going downstairs to have my breakfast, I see several young men with red flags in their hands standing in a line. I'm fairly certain that they're the executive members of the dormitory council. They stop every car leaving and call out, "Please vote!" They even say it to me as I pass by, though I don't have the right to vote here.

On the dorm bulletin board there's a company poster: "Let's all vote!" On the company bulletin board there's another poster made by the group sup-

---

* *Report of the Investigatory Commission on Seasonal Workers,* by the Educational Research Institute of Aomori Prefecture.

porting Watanabe, and also a radio and television schedule of all the candidates' campaign broadcasts, with the name of Watanabe written in big letters. Today's *Chunichi Daily* reports that the official election guidebooks (containing all the candidates' election speeches), which were supposed to be distributed personally to every voter, were discovered piled in the corner of the dining room of one dorm, and that someone protested to the National Election Administration Committee. But I see the same thing in our dining room.

Monday, December 11

This morning's *Chunichi* has this headline: "Once Again, Backed by the Toyota Group." Candidate Watanabe, former union president, has been elected in second place, with 101,229 votes. Miyata, another Social Democratic Party candidate in Fukuoka Prefecture, who was also the labor leader at the Shin-Nippon Steel Corporation* and supported jointly by the union and the company, was elected in the last qualifying place.

I still find lots of want-ads for seasonal workers. On the one hand, Toyota has experienced its second highest production in history, and on the other, it's extremely short of labor. No wonder, the work is so deadening. The attendance cards of the two new seasonal workers have been removed from the wallboard. The workers just disappeared. Miura says he saw them once in front of the lockers. As far as I can figure, six seasonal workers and three probationers have quit.

---

* The largest steel producer in Japan.

That leaves only three seasonal workers in my unit. Including the other shifts, fifteen or sixteen workers have quit.

Monday, December 11

I go to see Kudo in his workshop again. Workers scurry among the towering machines. When the blue-white welding light flashes in the dark building, I can see metallic dust drifting through the air. The noise, dust, and humidity are oppressive. The trolley conveyor moves through the shop, carrying all sorts of parts. Thirty-five years ago, workers must have seen the very same sight. Only now the machines are older, the building darker, and the working environment much worse.

Kudo races around inside his small work space—joining a drive shaft, turning it in the balancing machine, welding on small metal pieces to correct its weight, marking it, putting on oil and paint, lifting it and hanging it on the trolley conveyor. The last time I visited him, he looked at me and happily explained his work. He also had time to introduce me to the worker next to him. Today, he is moving things twice as fast as before and can't stop running.

I try to lift a drive shaft and can barely do it with both hands. Kudo, shorter than I, has to lift it higher than his eyes to hang it on the conveyor. Nine hundred shafts a day. I don't feel it's right to talk to him, and it doesn't seem polite to watch him work, so I leave. Without exaggeration, I must say he is doing the work of three people. I have never seen such quick motions. Kudo will come back after eight tomorrow morning, exhausted and pale, and he'll fall on an unmade bed without taking a bath. It's not surprising that he does nothing but sleep on Saturdays and Sundays.

Tuesday, December 12

I talk with Fukuyama, as we fit the rubbers on the speedometer shafts during overtime. "If we fail to produce our quota," I ask, "will the general foreman or the foreman be responsible for it?" "Neither," he says. "Here at Toyota, it's the workers' responsibility. They'll make us work until we finish the quota." Once, on the line, Iino complained that he had nothing to live for. I asked him, "If we rotate positions, would it help?" "No, as long as we're making transmissions, it's all the same." Even if we did rotate our positions on the line every other month, we'd soon learn everything about the job and again would hit that steel wall of monotony. It makes no difference whether you're assembling engines or drive shafts. As long as you're on the line, it's all the same.

Some call this labor, but we don't actually create anything. A single car can be disassembled into five or six thousand different parts, and it's the parts that now determine the organization of labor. Work is separated according to the function of the parts, then reorganized, framed, and fixed. A car is the integrated sum of all its parts, like a plastic model assembled in a fixed order, and we workers who assemble the parts are, in fact, controlled by the parts. Slowing the conveyor speed by five seconds might make the work easier for a while, but once we got used to this new speed, we'd again be trapped in the same narrow routine. They say that during World War II transmissions were carried by handcars and that bolts were tightened by hand screwdrivers. It sounds nice, but I doubt if the workers were any happier. Even if the work had wider variety and the production speed was left to the workers, the work was still fragmentary, lacking any sense of creation. On the line, we assemble mechanical parts in a mechanical way; our motions, dictated by the conveyor, are never far away from those of a machine.

I remember one of the bathroom graffiti: "Life is a battle against yourself." At first I took it as a general statement. But now I have a feeling that whoever wrote it must have felt that life itself is a conveyor.

My right wrist aches.

Wednesday, December 13
I go to see Yamamoto in his workshop. I had told him a few days ago that I wanted to visit his workshop and had asked where it was. He had answered, embarrassed, "There isn't much to see." Today he grimaces when he notices me. He's working among old, dusty machines, wearing dust-proof goggles. His ragged shirt is covered with yellow dust. He's pushing a cylinder block down a roller conveyor. Like an ancient Roman slave pulling a ship with a rope, he's straining with his back bent and his legs and arms taut.

Yamamoto works inside a narrow U-shaped space. His job is to push each cylinder block arriving from the foundry and to set it in the paring machine. When one machine finishes paring a cylinder, he removes it, changes its direction, pushes it on the roller conveyor, and then sets it in another machine. After switching on the second machine—and without being able to watch the operation—he walks to another machine, which he has already turned on; here, he pushes a pared cylinder block to yet another machine, sets it in, turns a switch, and returns to the second machine, takes a block off, moves it on . . . endless repetition of this. All the while, too, he works with a hammer and a driver. He's responsible for nine machines and has to finish ninety-four blocks a day. He does what a transfer machine does, or more accurately, he replaces a transfer machine.

Saturday, December 16
My fingers are stiff. I massage them on my way to work. Tonight while I'm washing my clothes, Yamamoto drops by. He didn't go to work today and tells me that Saito, his roommate from Fukuoka who wanted to join the Self-Defense Forces, quit yesterday and returned home. Though Saito only had a week left in his contract and would have received his bonus had he stayed, he simply couldn't stand the work at the foundry any longer. "I don't talk with the regular workers," Yamamoto says. The seasonal workers despise the regular workers, wondering how they can stand the work, and the regular workers despise the seasonal workers as "migrants."

Lately Hashimoto has begun skipping work. His wife's pregnant, and he wants to be with her. There aren't enough workers on the line, and during lunch break there were a lot of complaints, a sign of built-up fatigue. One fellow said that our shift had two less workers than any other shift. At Toyota, if production increases with fewer workers, the general foreman receives a high rating because of cost reduction. Someone else complained, "The machines in our transmission shop are all secondhand from other shops."

It's not just our shop. One day Kudo returned from work and exclaimed, "They put us in the most difficult positions one after another. Hayashi, who's a regular worker, has a better balancing machine; the safety device responds as soon as he presses the pedal. But mine doesn't. Mine works too slow, which is very dangerous. Today I passed three shafts without balancing."

Someone else suggested that they should put in four or five people specified as daylight-shift workers who could work overlapping the first and second shifts and increase the line speed a little during that time, so the second shift wouldn't have to work until two or three in the morning. A good idea, but one that would surely be rejected by the management. There are lots of complaints, but they never get far. Nobody suggests taking these grievances to the union. Nobody seems to remember that a union is an organization for solving problems.

Sunday, December 17

Friday, the *Toyota* ran an article headlined, "This Year's Output to Top Two Million." It reported:

> This record production is the result of the effort and originality of the 200,000 people of the Toyota group, not only the 42,000 Toyota employees but also those in its affiliated companies and suppliers as well as dealers. This figure shows the firm confidence of the numerous customers who have chosen Toyota cars. And this year as well, our company will continue to maintain its position as the third largest automobile manufacturer in the world.

Last night Yamamoto came to say goodbye. On the twenty-fifth his contract will be up. His hair had been cut and he looked neat. After he returns home, he hopes to get his driver's licence and find a white-collar job in an office. He smiled as he told me, "I'll never come back here."

Yamamoto also told me that a trainee in his workshop got his finger caught in a machine the week before. In Kudo's workshop, a seasonal worker on the other shift had a finger crushed, and in my workshop, too, a worker on the other shift lost a finger. The strange thing is that no news about these accidents is ever published. We learn about them only by word of mouth. Even when a worker dies, management simply announces that there has been a "serious accident." There's never a word of apology or condolence for fingers cut off, arms chopped off, or legs crushed.

Monday, December 18
I get my pay slip. Three days off for sickness. Basic pay with production allowance: $163.41. Total wages including overtime and overnight allowances: $230.10. Take-home pay: $220.00. It's not much. Still, everybody is in a good mood on paydays. We always talk about our bad wages, but with the large overtime and overnight allowances, the total is endurable. Our wages are slightly better than those in other industries in the area, though we also work much longer and harder. All this, in turn, helps reinforce our reliance on the company. Just when you might think of quitting, you remember your wages and forget how hard you have to work to earn them. And many of us are already thinking about monthly installments on the car, the color TV, the stereo, or the house. Kudo buys things as if he were exacting revenge for something.

He buys things in a strange fever. For instance, he bought a watch and then just locked it away in the closet.

From the moment a worker passes through the company gate and shows his identification card to the guard, he exists only as a number. He checks his mind and heart in the cloakroom along with his coat. Only when he leaves ten or twelve hours later can he retrieve his identity, individual dignity, and personality. Looking around me, I realize that the workers in this automobile factory literally work like slaves. What crimes have we committed to be punished with such hard labor?

Today a young boy of under eighteen arrived. He was smiling.

Tuesday, December 19

When it gets close to starting time, everybody glances at the time clock. We always check to see if there are any cards left. Today, two cards are left unmarked. Fukuyama and Hashimoto don't turn up. The foreman and the team chief take their places on the line. There are no relief men. At eleven the line stops for five minutes to allow us to go to the toilet, which is quite exceptional. Everyone is tired and jumpy. Before the break, a cover had failed to fit smoothly, and I had thrown it on the floor in anger. Even Takeda, usually quite calm, had thrown some balky bolts onto the other side of the line. We all get irritated when parts don't fit smoothly. Sometimes, out of frustration, I take a great swipe with the hammer and catch my own hand on the follow-through and don't know whether to laugh or cry.

By ten this evening I'm exhausted. Starting at 12:30

A.M. we're supposed to do an hour of overtime to prepare for tomorrow, but I stop working after about thirty minutes and leave. Takeda also stops, and we come back together. He says the work is just too "stupid." "I'd love to win the first prize in a lottery!" he says. "If I did, I could live on the interest. Then I could choose a job where I could get plenty of holidays and go mountain climbing whenever I liked. That's my dream."

In the morning, one of the team chiefs in my work section has the third finger of his right hand cut off at the first joint. The general foreman makes a speech: "There's no point in blaming anyone for what happened. But be careful, otherwise you'll inconvenience the others. They'll have to do your job as well as their own." Nobody has a word about the pain of the injured man. In fact, everybody was sympathetic to the section manager for having a run of bad luck with accidents in his shop. The general foreman and the team chief are only concerned about how the accident affects their records. The *Municipal Administration Study Monthly* (September 5, 1970) reports:

> If an accident occurs, the ones responsible for the group have their next bonus (given every six months) reduced: 40 percent for the team chief, 30 percent for the foreman, 20 percent for the general foreman and 10 percent for the section manager.

The team chief glances at his Safety First arm band and mumbles that he won't be able to take it off for some time now. Because of this accident, our shop will be a "Designated Safety Campaign Shop" for another three months, with more meetings after work, which nobody likes. If management wants to prevent more accidents, they should install better machines or at least let us work at a normal pace.

Wednesday, December 20

Kudo tells me that the injured man was the team chief on the other shift in his workshop. The accident had happened only thirty minutes before the shift change. Pressed for time, the man had been operating two machines at once, and his hand got caught in one of them. Obviously, the accident was caused by the pressure to work faster. According to Kudo, the general foreman said that he would give the man proper indemnity because he cheerfully apologized to the section manager instead of making complaints. At Toyota, the victim has to apologize! Kudo mentions all this nonchalantly and adds, "He was lucky, he only lost a finger."

Today's target is 461 boxes. The line works until 12:45 A.M. It is 2:30 when I return to the dorm, and I wake up at 8:30 when Kudo comes back. On the second shift, I sleep only six hours. The workers with young children sleep even less.

Thursday, December 21

Overtime on the line until 12:50 A.M. We refill our boxes with new parts for ten minutes and fit rubbers on the speedometer shafts for yet another thirty minutes. It's three in the morning when I get back. Five-and-a-half hours continuous work on the line, from 7:15 to 12:50—a full day's worth of ordinary work. After ten, I wasn't able to put anything into my work. During the break, everybody seemed exhausted. Murayama, who threw up after supper, lay on a bench looking very sick. "Why the hell is production increasing so much?" he asked weakly. "Because the cars sell well," someone answered. "There's a lot of land reclamation going on," someone said, "so they need a lot of trucks."

This evening, the foreman handed out a leaflet published by the Personnel Department entitled "To Those Who Are Leaving." It read:

Please talk about Toyota to your parents and your friends, as you eat rice cakes together. And be sure to show them "A Guide to Toyota." You can help company public relations by introducing the type of friends about whom you think:
- He'll understand me during hard times.
- I wonder what he's doing now?
- I'd like to get him to join us and work together with us.

Or, if you know someone like the following, please recommend him:
- Prospective graduates from high schools next spring or those who graduated less than two years ago.
- Prospective graduates from vocational training schools.
- Members of the Self-Defense Forces who are expected to complete their terms or who completed them less than three months ago.
- Probationers between the ages of sixteen and forty-seven.
- Seasonal workers between eighteen and fifty who can work for more than three months.

And at the bottom of the leaflet there is a detachable recommendation form.

There were many comments:

"Which 'company' do they mean?"

"Hey, if it's this good, I might apply myself."

"If I introduce somebody, will they pay me something?"

"Yeah. They'll give you ten dollars."

"It's not worth it. I don't want to make anybody hold a grudge against me all my life for ten dollars."

Before we could talk any more, the line started moving again. Murayama bent over and threw up again beside the line. There were no relief men around.

"Anyone can recognize a Toyota worker right away," the saying here goes. "He's thin and pale and his eyes are red."

On my way back I met an old man I have often seen in the dorm dining room. I said hello, and we walked together talking. He said he was working in the building next to mine. He's from Hokkaido and was a seasonal worker at Nissan for the last six years, but this year they rejected him because of albumin in his urine.

Kudo's in a bad mood these days, very sullen. He's not feeling well and lately has been taking medicine his hospital back home sends him. I'm worried that the head injury he got in that traffic accident is bothering him again.

Friday, December 22

Two people don't show up, so there are no relief men again. I work until 12:50. Iino says that our target yesterday was 510 boxes. Today it must be the same. Production has increased to 785 boxes a day without our realizing it. That's 140 boxes more than when I started. No one knows how late we'll work each night or how many boxes we'll have to produce. Each of us is merely following orders from a computerized control room. A tape tells us how many boxes we have to put on the line for the final-assembly plant the next morning.

Whenever we get together these days, all we talk about is the changing of the working shifts. There's a rumor that next year the present two-shift system, in which one shift immediately follows the other, will be dropped for separate day and night shifts, with some hours in between. But no official announcement has yet been made. The foreman himself hasn't received any information. The projected system is designed to get more overtime out of everyone, and most of us are against it, but as someone said, "If it's official management policy, then there's nothing we can do about it." The rumor is upsetting, but it's difficult to fight against a rumor. Management is following a very clever psychological strategy. Even a basic change of working conditions such as this won't be discussed in or by the labor union. In fact, nobody mentions the labor union at all. It's as if the union doesn't exist.

Around five this morning, my wife went by herself to the hospital. She's been worried about having a premature birth. I'm very worried about my family. There are still three working days left before the end of the year, but I've decided to go home.

5

UNTIL THE LINE STOPS

Sunday, January 7, 1973

There is a New Year's party at the hotel near the dormitory. The hotel—it's more like an inn—has a tower in front with a real car on top. I'm the only seasonal worker at the party.

The foreman begins the party with a speech. He announces that this year we'll produce 800 boxes a day, and that there will also be more overtime. He ends his speech by saying, "Please be careful and don't get injured. I'm counting on your collaboration."

After a while they start to party it up. Some pour *sake* all around, some sing pop songs over a microphone, and some dance with the waitresses. No one gets drunk. I was expecting someone to get angry or talk about his frustrations, but they are very discreet. After the party, everyone plays mah-jongg in the other room. Not knowing the rules, Takeda and I go to a nearby coffee shop. Finally we walk back to the dorm in the rain.

Work started again on January 5, but there are still four or five guys who haven't reported for work yet.

Monday, January 8

My first day on the night shift. I work from 9:00 P.M. until 6:00 A.M. It's worst between four and five. Tired as I am, I keep on assembling parts, following the rhythm of the line, thinking only about going to bed and sleeping as soon as I can.

117

When I get out of the workshop, I see a glow behind the mountains in the east. I eat breakfast at the main canteen, though I fall asleep from time to time. On the way back, I meet Kudo coming to work. Last night on my way to work, I met him at almost the same place.

Tuesday, January 9

A clear bright day. I don't want to draw the curtains and go to sleep. I never get to see the world any more.

This morning's conversation in front of the lockers:

"When I'm on the night shift, I get morning erections. My pants hurt."

"It's not a morning erection. It's fatigue. A morning erection is a sign of good health, but yours is no good."

"Who in hell invented night shifts?"

In the *Toyota* of January 1, the president, Eiji Toyota, was reported as saying: "I hope we can fulfill our plan to produce 1,550,000 cars for the domestic market and 800,000 for export, a total of 2,350,000 cars, and an increase of 12 percent."

The working system has changed three times in six months. Until August, there was a single daytime shift. From September to December there were two shifts, a day shift and an evening shift immediately following it. Now there is a day-night shift system that allows the company to get the workers to work lots of overtime on both shifts. And the management never consulted the workers in any way before making these changes. They increased production without increasing the number of workers simply by requiring more overtime work.

Wednesday, January 10

I'm exhausted and so cold and sleepy that I barely make it back to the dorm. During our break, I could see that everyone was shivering. There are only two steam radiators in our flimsy plastic-paneled locker room. One worker said, with his teeth rattling, "Have you read today's paper? They made one hundred million dollars profit! And that's net profit! They earn six or seven hundred thousand dollars a day by making us work in this hole."

He usually has something sharp and to the point to say about the company, but no one continued the conversation. After a while someone said, "We'll see what they say when it comes time for the next pay raise. I bet they'll say their situation is 'very severe' or something like that again. The union's no good because it just makes excuses for the company. The only time the union really gets to work is when there's an election."

On January 8, the Toyota Motor Company announced that its net profit in the half-yearly statement (from June through November 1972) was $106,483,000. This is the first time in Japanese history that a company has made a profit exceeding $100 million. Toyota set the previous record in the last statement with a net profit of $85,600,000. This beat out the Matsushita Electric Company (Panasonic), and Toyota has remained in first place for two consecutive terms.

At dawn, the team chief came to me and helped me for a while. "Don't you want to stay with Toyota?" he said.

"No, the work's too tough . . ."

"You have character. I'm willing to recommend you."

He said some other things, but I couldn't hear what they were, since I was working and the cleaning machines, motors, air hammers, and impactors were too loud.

From today, the production target is 400 boxes per shift. The financial statement for the period ending in November says that the company invested $54 million in securities and that Toyota's total investments will reach $70 million. They also reserved $211 million for special depreciation and $43 million for the development of overseas markets. The company has enormous reserves and allowances, which they use to accumulate capital and which help them minimize their published profit. They'll appropriate $283 million ($167 million more than last year) for buying land for factories, for factory construction, and for plant modernization. Meanwhile, on the floor we're shivering.

Between 1968 and 1972, units sold, sales volume, and net profit all doubled, while the number of workers increased by only 20 percent. Although car units sold increased by 75,000 and profit by $22,260,000 between the biannual accounting periods ending in May and November of 1972, the number of workers decreased by 191!

Thursday, January 11

When I went to work last night, I knew immediately something was wrong. The team chief on the other shift stood there rather uneasily, and the workers who had just arrived surrounded him. I asked Miura, who

120

works with me, if there had been an accident. He said that Kawamura, a seasonal worker, had been severely shocked. Kawamura is a young man from Hokkaido, where he worked as a carpenter. They carried him to the Toyota Hospital, and he'll probably be there for more than a week.

Before work started, the general foreman made one of his little speeches: "Kawamura's biorhythm chart shows that today is his worst day. Looks like the chart was right!"

The workers knew the real story. Going to get some parts he needed, Kawamura crossed over two small conveyor belts and touched a machine. But the machine (a parts feeder that fits washers in bolts) was so old that some of a 200-volt electric cord was frayed. And his gloves were wet. He received a severe shock and fell to the floor. He suffered a concussion and lost consciousness. Luckily the current passed through the base of his finger. If it had gone near his heart, he would have been killed instantly.

On the day of the accident, his team was short of workers, since two people hadn't showed up and one seasonal worker had quit. Superficially, the cause of the accident was that he took a shortcut to get the parts, but the real cause was the short circuit in the old machine, and also, the fact that there was no bridge over the line. But according to the general foreman (who's also a member of the union!), the problem was in the worker's biorhythm, and the key to safety is for all of us to be careful when our own biorhythms are bad.

This year's new slogan is written on the company's blackboard: "Whatever you do, be prepared to take responsibility for it."

Friday, January 12

At dawn we are still working in the cold, shivering. Our overtime on the line lasts until 7:15 A.M. I hear that the pace of the line has been changed to one minute and sixteen seconds. That's four seconds faster than when I started in September.

Tuesday, January 16

An endless flow of cases. "Until the line stops" is what I keep telling myself, but that seems a very long time. When I got to work last night, I found a steel stairway installed over the subline. It was painted bright yellow. We had been demanding a stairway in our workshop for a long time. It makes me angry to think that Kawamura had to get shocked before they'd put it in.

I come back with Ogi, whom we call "Red Line" because of the red stripe on his cap indicating that he's a minor. He says he was born in 1956, so he's sixteen. I feel a little strange working with a kid twenty years younger than I am, doing the same work. He tells me that he graduated from junior high school last March and worked with his family in Miyazaki until he came to Toyota. His family makes tombstones. Kudo used to make Buddhist family altars. What a weird coincidence! As for the others, Ota comes from Tokushima and used to be a joiner. The two guys from Hokkaido were carpenters. It's getting harder and harder to be a craftsman. Ogi tells me they used to chisel tombstones by hand, but now they use machines. Even craftsmen need capital, and if orders are scarce, they have to become factory workers.

Ogi says that the canteen food gives him indigestion. The first week he came, he vomited every day. Even now when he starts working at the line after a meal, he soon asks the team chief to relieve him and goes to the toilet to vomit. He says his stomach usually hurts. I wonder how long it will take for his face to turn pale and lose its liveliness. He never complains that he's tired or that the work is hard. He says that he expected to work on the line and that he finds it neither pleasant nor hard. He seems comforted by believing that his work is the easiest of all. When I ask him how he likes the night shift, he just says, "I get sleepy." Then he adds, "When I had my interview with a guy from Toyota at the Public Employment Security Office, he didn't mention the night shift at all."

I had thought it was illegal to make a sixteen-year-old kid work past midnight. In the 1830s England had already prohibited people under eighteen from working at night. Now, we're supposedly working in a "modern" factory!

Wednesday, January 17
Downtown I run across a law book at a bookstore. In the Labor Standards Law, I find:

NIGHT LABOR

ARTICLE 62. The employer shall not employ minors under 18 years of age or women between the hours of 10 P.M. and 5 A.M. *However, this shall not apply if the male over 16 years of age is employed on a shift system.*

At work, more graffiti. Somebody wrote "Screw the night shift!" in chalk on a bench by the locker-room wall. A worker is reading a *Toyota Weekly* he's picked up from the bench. "Not for us," he says. "It's not for us. There's nothing in here for us." The newspaper is mainly a revised list of business-trip and commuting expense allowances.

At the meeting before work, the team chief calls my name and hands me a "smile" button with the Toyota trademark on it. According to him, today is supposed to be my "bad day." He tells me to be careful. The general foreman checked our birthdays, calculated our bad days, and made a list. As I put the button on my work cap next to my number badge, I'm embarrassed. Since Kawamura's accident, the biorhythm safety campaign is really being pushed. Although it might be my "bad day," I feel better than usual.

I get my pay slip. Three absences. Basic pay, including the production allowance: $164.07. Total wages: $230.97. Take-home pay: $219. This month I'll send $170 home.

Thursday, January 18

They say we made 425 boxes today. Though we have no time to count, our production has increased by 25 boxes a day. Soon we'll be making 450 boxes a day. When I get back tonight, I find Kudo still there.

"Aren't you going to work?"

"No, not today. Not tomorrow, either."

"Are you feeling bad?"

"I'm leaving. Today I fell on the floor unconscious," he says, looking at me weakly.

Last night he worked the night shift, but as soon as he started, he felt sick. He tried to keep on working. When he checked the clock, it was 12:50 A.M. Ten minutes to go until the break for the midnight meal. When he looked at the clock again, three minutes had passed. Seven more minutes, he thought, and then he fell on the floor. When he came to he was lying on a bench, covered with the coat he had just bought. Someone must have opened his locker and put it over him. The foreman, who was standing beside him, told him that right after he fell, they had carried him to the Toyota Hospital, just outside the factory grounds. They had given him an injection, and then he had been transferred to the infirmary inside the factory. It was already morning when he came to. Why hadn't they left him to sleep in a soft hospital bed?

When he was carried to the hospital again, Kudo told them about the traffic accident he'd had before. The general foreman told Kudo, "Once you fall, you can't work any more. I'll see that your account is settled. Rest well at home, and then come and see us again." That was all; he was fired.

"At least I'm glad I'm alive," Kudo adds. "Well, I won't worry. Anyway, they need someone at home to shovel the snow off the roof. It's only forty-six days till the end of my contract, though. Then I could have gotten my bonus." His voice becomes choked with emotion and he can't talk any more.

I recall how he worked from eight to eight, but he reported to the shop an hour early to prepare for work, wash parts, and melt wax. He wasn't paid for these jobs, but without doing them he wouldn't have been able to keep up with his work. He's a real craftsman. He wants to do his job well. Both of us just sit looking at each other for a while, and finally he speaks: "I'm feeling much better. I could go to work right now."

Friday, January 19

At the gate, they're handing out a special issue of *Toyota Weekly*. It's a report on yesterday's labor-management conference on the five-day work week system. The president of the committee, Mr. Umebayashi, is quoted as saying:

> Since work has become both intensive and monotonous due to rapid mechanization, we must develop a new sense of worth in work to cope with it. Therefore, we demand the harmonization of work and leisure.
>
> Since Toyota has developed rapidly and has entered into fair competition with overseas companies, and because international opinion has also asked us to establish proper and fair working conditions, the question of the five-day work week system must be faced up to and must be solved as quickly as possible by labor and management.

To this, President Toyota replied:

> The five-day work week is an important question that is closely related to the basic principles of management. So we must give it sufficient consideration.
>
> This year (1) sales competition will be more severe, and we cannot be optimistic about sales both in Japan and overseas; (2) we will be asked to use efficient antipollution devices; (3) we must produce and sell 2,350,000 cars by all means in order to stay in first place; and (4) we want to make this year the start of our overseas expansion.
>
> We have many problems and are in a difficult situation, so I want you to understand how difficult it is to introduce a system that would affect our very viability as a business.

No one in the workshop pays any attention to these handouts. The five-day work week has already been discussed, and they expect it to be instituted in April.

It was the same when night and day shifts were introduced: no one did anything to protest it. They had expected it would be put into effect in January even before they were officially told. Workers didn't think it was something to negotiate. As for a five-day work week, they don't imagine that they can present demands or go on strike. They take it for granted that it will be decided by the top and sent down. Then again, many of them are thinking that whatever happens, it won't make much difference.

Saturday, January 20

When I awake this morning, Kudo is gone. On my way to work, I see him walking along with his coat hood pulled up over his head. He says he's been to the workshop to get his belongings.

When I come back to the room, he's already left with his younger brother, who came down from Tokyo. Kudo has left a note tacked to the door: "Thank you for everything. Sorry that I didn't see you when I left. Good luck. Hiroshi." In the room I find a piece of cardboard on which he has written with a felt-tipped pen: "Dear Satoshi, you've got only one month left. Take care of yourself. Hoping you'll make it. Please excuse me for going first. Hiroshi."

Anger is boiling up inside me, and I can't force it down. Kudo pushed himself to the limit to get his money, and once he was unable to work, the company just threw him out. He's gone home with a disease like a time bomb inside him. No compensation, even. Kudo has left the calendar he got from the electrical appliance store in front of the dorm. He put the hours he worked under each date: On January 8, for example, he wrote, "from 8:00 to 8:00," and on January 9,

127

"from 8:00 to 7:30." And starting on January 16, he began to write in big letters the number of days till the end of his contract. Under March 15, he wrote "The End of My Contract" in capital letters. He was looking forward to the end of his contract day by day, thinking only of going home with the $77 bonus. And so am I. I'm marking the days left on the wall calendar beside my bed with a ball-point pen.

Monday, January 22

The *Toyota* headlines the promotion ceremony for probationers: "With Burning Determination. 91 Men!" I think 91 people in three months is a small number. Last October 13, 126 were promoted—and I think only 400 people became regular workers last year. The rest must have quit. Whenever I see want-ads in the paper, I think instead of the people who are leaving.

Tuesday, January 23

Back on the night shift. As the sun rises, you can see the blue outlines of skylights in the serrated roof of the factory. To someone looking down through those skylights, the workshop must look like the bottom of the sea. The shapes of workers moving here and there, rushing across the bottom, must look like fish in an aquarium. The floor of the factory is lit with fluorescent lamps, and the sun's rays haven't begun to shine in yet. The morning light comes in gradually, and the factory gets slowly lighter. Numb with fatigue, you move your lips as if trying to inhale the faint sunlight.

I come back with Takeda and Ogi. "There are many kinds of lives, aren't there?" says Takeda. "I was watching TV the other day and saw a man who wanders around searching for a supposedly extinct Japanese wolf."

"Yeah, I saw it too," says Ogi, nodding. Then Takeda adds in a rather cynical tone, "Our work is like that, only we're running after transmissions every day."

"No, it's not the same," I say. "We're the ones who are being chased." What does this nineteen-year-old boy think about at work? Does he ever ask himself, "Can this work I do every day be called a life? What kind of life am I living? What kind of life should I live?"

Wednesday, January 24

We have made 440 boxes. The line moves until 7:30 A.M. The break after the night meal ends at 1:30, so I have worked for six hours without resting. I have a feeling that this speed-up will continue from now on. After 6:00 A.M., I fall behind. Production is being increased little by little, and we're pushed harder and harder to fill our quota. I take sleeping pills since I can't sleep during the day. If I take several pills, I can sleep from 10:00 A.M. to 5:00 P.M., but I can't shake off my fatigue. After eating our night meal at the break, everyone sits close on the bench, exhausted and talking in low voices. Our talk doesn't sound as lively as it used to.

"Normal people are sleeping now, aren't they?" someone says.

"We're normal, too. It's the president who's making us abnormal."

"No, you're wrong! You've been here for seven years. That means you've already become abnormal."

"The only thing I still enjoy is *sake*."

129

"When I'm on the night shift, my *sake* goes fast."

"I can't keep a big bottle three days."

"When I get home, I have one glass before going to bed, another glass when I wake after two or three hours, and another just before going to work to kill the depression."

Today there is a cease-fire in Vietnam.

Thursday, January 25

Very warm and raining today. An hour after starting work, I'm already exhausted and feel like going home. I think I can only continue until the night meal, but after I fall into the work rhythm, I manage to work until morning.

Around six in the evening, as I'm sleeping in my curtained room, the dormitory supervisor unlocks the door and comes in. He says that a seasonal worker is due to arrive tomorrow. Once before, too, I found a supervisor in my room when I came back from the bath. I'm worried that he has seen my books, though I'm very careful about that. Why should they have the right to enter my room without my permission? They always find some excuse, but the truth is that to them the dormitory seems like a warehouse where they keep their human merchandise, which they check from time to time.

Friday, January 26

The line stops at seven this morning. The general foreman asks me, "How about working one more month? We'll be very busy in March." From March, the production target will be 900 boxes a day, 100 more than what we're straining to produce now.

They've hired 900 high school graduates, but the new workers won't arrive until the end of March. And the seasonal workers are beginning to go home to their farms.

"We appreciate your good work," the general foreman tells me. "Can't you stay a little longer?"

"I'll think about it," I say, and leave. I'm in no mood to stay. Right now we have to do an hour overtime just to produce 400 boxes on a single shift. If they increase output by 50 boxes, we'll have to do at least another hour of overtime.

During the night break, the team chief told us there was an accident in the gear workshop: a worker crushed his left thumb. Everyone started to talk about accidents. "At Toyota," one worker said, "we often hear about accidents—one guy was killed and another was injured. But we never hear that the line's been stopped because of it."

"They make more money with higher production even though one or two men will die."

"We rush through the same thing day after day, so there are bound to be accidents."

"A lot of the team chiefs and foremen have no hands, you know."

"I know a foreman who lost the fingers from both hands. He can't even wash his face."

"I know a guy who lost his face! He fell on a press and got his chin caught in it."

"One guy was cleaning a forging machine during the lunch break, and when he switched it on afterwards, he found some arms and fingers. They checked, and a worker was missing."

We exchanged stories until one, when the line

131

started again. Then we all stood up and someone mumbled, "Well, back to work."

"Well," someone else said, "let's go back down to hell."

Saturday, January 27

Around six in the evening, a new roommate arrives to replace Kudo. I realize that I'm one of the old-timers in the shop and dorm now. The new guy, Kiichi Hamada, is thirty-four years old, small and quiet. He has a boy who will enter elementary school this year and a five-year-old girl. He's a farmer from the south, from Itsuki village in Kumamoto Prefecture. He worked in the Self-Defense Air Force in Ashiya until five years ago. After that, he worked three winters as a seasonal worker in Osaka and Tokyo. He's come to Toyota because his younger brother, who's also an ex–military man, is already here, and because in a big company he can be sure of getting paid. "The meals in the Air Force," he said, "are much better than they are here."

On my way to work I meet Ota and Miura.

"What did the general foreman say to you yesterday?"

"I can't tell you," I kid them, "because it was really juicy."

"I'll bet he said, in a nice sweet voice, 'Don't you want to be a regular worker? You've been doing real fine.' "

"Well, not far from it." I can't keep from laughing at his imitation. "He asked me to stay one more month, because they're increasing production again in March."

"Again? We're in the same boat as the young girls

who worked as spinners in sweatshops fifty or sixty years ago. Someone should write about us the same way they wrote about them, and call it *Cruel Tales of Toyota*. I bet it would be a best-seller."

Then suddenly one of them says, "You look very pale in the mornings." I'm shocked, because I've been anemic for weeks and can hardly keep standing until morning, but I didn't think anyone would notice. Recently, I've been feeling ill after I eat my night meal. But if I don't eat a regular meal, a bowl of noodles at least, I can't keep going.

When we arrive at the workshop, we see a notice on the blackboard: "All factory workers are expected to report for work on February 10 and 17, March 3 and 10." These are all Saturdays, which the night shift usually has off. If we work on the Saturday night shift, we return on Sunday morning and have to report again on Monday morning. There isn't enough time to rest.

"Is this somebody's idea of a joke?" someone says. Nobody laughs.

"When did they decide this?" Everybody looks completely taken aback and at a loss for words.

"Has the union agreed to this?"

"I bet they bought off the union with some women at that night club . . ." Nobody laughs at this, either. Everyone is really anxious. Murayama, our shop steward, telephones the union, and they tell him they have just received the company's proposal and are discussing it. Everybody is resigned: "They'll probably agree to it." But it isn't a question of the union agreeing or disagreeing. There it is, presented in the form of an order on the blackboard. The decision was made long ago.

During the break, everybody gathers around the radiator and reads the *Toyota*. The company paper is well edited and widely read. On top of the front page there's a quote from the president's speech at the shareholders' general meeting: "In step with research developments and with the rationalization of management, we will raise sales to about $2 billion in 1973."

Below this are quotes from another speech the president made at the general meeting of the Auto Dealers' Association, which consists of 275 members. There are also a group of photos of the president, captioned: "Onward United! Let's Sell 1,550,000 Cars!" And Mr. Toyota is quoted: "This year we will further consolidate our leadership in the domestic market. The dealers, Toyota Motor Sales Company, and Toyota Motor Company must all unite and strive to defeat our competitors."

At the same meeting Mr. Kamiya, president of the Toyota Motor Sales Company said, "Let's hold on to our top position with all our might."

We talk as we read the paper.

"They say they're going to hire a lot of college graduates. They're just increasing nonproductive members. What good will they be?"

"You can find a lot of them in the coffee shops."

"Yeah, they work hard at bowling."

"This is the computer age, isn't it? Why don't they throw them out and let the computer do all the office work?"

"And send them to the workshop!"

"Yeah, and let the president take care of the office work by himself." We all laugh hard at this.

"But cutting down the nonproductive jobs won't help much. They'd still keep speeding up the line by two or three seconds. That's how they make the money."

"If all the guys here quit so soon, it's the company that loses in the end, isn't it?"

"No. If the workers stay here two or three months, that's long enough for the company. Even after they pay for travel and the ads, the company still gains."

"Just look around. There aren't any fat guys at Toyota. You'll see when you go to the bath. Our bodies all look the same. Sick and pale."

"You'll lose ten or fifteen pounds while you're at Toyota. The guys who quit and went to work for another company all have fat faces now."

"It won't be long before the company goes into the funeral business."

"They're making fools of us . . ."

Monday, January 29

Even the littlest thing at work tires me. Each individual motion of my work doesn't look hard; it's the repetition and the monotony that exhaust you.

Although the many workers here are closely connected by the object they are making and are working in such close proximity, our vision is restricted to an area of one square yard. We spend long hours without speaking even a word to the next worker. When we get back to the dorm, our roommates have already gone to work on the other shift. The more the company "rationalizes production," the lonelier we workers become. And the more alienated we become, the more we fall back on our families and try to find fulfillment in leisure. The main topics of conversation at the shop are usually the average bowling scores or where people went out driving.

This morning, at ten to eight, the general foreman makes his usual speech. About thirty workers, including some from the processing shop who belong to a different team, have to attend.

"Starting in March we have to make 890 boxes a day. In order to do this, I have to ask you to work two extra days both in February and in March. In April we'll probably go back to 790 boxes. Now, you may ask why we don't carry over some production to April. Well, our customers say they want their cars in March. If the cars aren't ready by then, they'll go and get Datsuns. So for the time being, I want you to do your best and not take holidays. Each of you is responsible for our production. And each of you is responsible for quality, too. Remember, I want you to do your best."

The line moves without stopping from the start of the work till the end. If there is a company announcement, a speech by the management on quality control, or a lecture on safety, we have to listen to it during unpaid overtime. And since the line moves for all our work time, we also have to replenish parts and make up for delays outside of work hours. And in order to change our clothes, have a smoke, or go to the toilet, we have to arrive before starting time. Then we stand in front of the line waiting for work to start, like runners waiting for the signal gun to fire.

Suppose that the management steals at least fifteen minutes a day of our time before work, during the break, and after work. There are twenty-two working days a month, which means five-and-a-half hours a month stolen from us. In plants where the rules are even stricter, or the bosses like making speeches, or the workers are unskilled, the company would steal more than ten hours a month.

Tuesday, January 30

Ogi comes back at four-thirty because he has a stomach ache. It's the young workers like Ogi who give the biggest profit to the company. At Toyota, pay is based on age. According to the ads in the paper, they offer a sixteen-year-old male $155 a month (excluding overtime) and a forty-seven-year-old male $308 (for working on the two-shift system with twenty-five hours of overtime).

Wednesday, January 31

The end of January. Twelve more days till the end of my contract, and I'm pretty worn out. It seems a miracle to me that I've lasted until today. The line keeps moving, faster and faster.

At work, I can't fit an idler shaft in smoothly, and it really bothers me. In the afternoon, more parts give me difficulty. I have to fight frustration all the way. They say we've made 436 boxes by 6:15 P.M.

I come back with Iino. He has some interesting things to say:

The rice at the canteen tastes so bad because the cooks just steam it. It gets puffy, but it's still dry and undercooked. It's very bad for our digestion. Until recently, they served rice mixed with barley.

Our general foreman will soon be promoted to section manager. Since he started as an ordinary worker in the shop, everyone will be "encouraged" to work harder in order to be given the same privilege.

Ogi can't become a regular worker until he turns eighteen, another two years, no matter how hard he works.

They didn't always make transmissions for the PH and KM models on our line. But some guy suggested that they could be made here, and so orders were withdrawn from a subcontracting company and forced on us. Our line isn't designed to handle them—it's far too short. The guy who suggested this idea was promoted and transferred somewhere else.

6

FREEDOM

Thursday, February 1

It's finally February! One more month to go. Today our general foreman is promoted to assistant section manager. He's going to leave the shop floor and sit in the office. People have started calling him all sorts of names. They're getting back because he used them as stepping stones to his own promotion.

The *Chunichi Daily* newspaper devotes eight columns to reporting all the personnel changes. It looks like an auto-industry trade paper. Toyota's clearly the biggest thing around here. Among the changes, I find something called "transfer to Toyota Cooperative." It seems strange that a company is officially sending personnel to a consumer cooperative. The cooperative openly prints slogans put out by the Toyota City police office on the front and inside page of its news bulletin. For example, "This is the age of speed. Send information on criminals directly to the police." People say that there are two former police chiefs at Toyota.

Friday, February 2

During the lunch break the newly promoted managerial staff is introduced. With a portable microphone in his hand, a department manager makes a short speech on the windy factory floor. Red with excitement, the general foreman speaks from a platform: "I am grateful for the kind guidance given me by the manager and my other superiors. I also would like to thank you for your help." As soon as it's over, the nearly hundred of us who are there rush to the canteen.

Saturday, February 3

Yoshizaki is going to Kyushu next weekend. The Personnel Department is sending him to recruit from the Self-Defense Forces. Probably, he was chosen because he himself is an ex–military man. Everyone is envious because the workers on the shop floor never take business trips. A few complained that while he's away we'll be a hand short on the line. Two of the men in my group are ex-military, and so are Hamada, my new roommate, and his brother. There are several former military men on the shop floor, especially among the guards, dormitory supervisors, and those in charge of personnel training. They are hired as regular employees, and the time they spent in the military is even counted as seniority. The company seems to favor them in every respect.

There is even a special military recruiting office in Toyota City, and it's very active. Its posters are up all along the road to the factory, and attached to each are application cards to fill in. Iino, who lives with a former military man, told me that he saw a Toyota want-ad in the Self-Defense Forces *Bulletin*. "It's strange," he said with a puzzled look. "It's clear that they're helping each other."

The November issue of the *Military Research Monthly* ran an article by Osamu Inagaki called "The Active Role of Ex–Military Men at Toyota." Essentially, it's a report written by the recruiting section of the company's Personnel Department. It points out that Toyota was "the first company to support and

142

cooperate with the Ground Forces" and that, since November 1961, it has directly employed the discharged soldiers as regular employees. A newly employed person who is not a recent school graduate normally has to wait six months to a year before he becomes a regular employee, but an ex–military man is not only employed as a "regular" employee from the start but is promoted to team chief within five or six years while others take more than nine years.

Today there are 2,500 former military men in Toyota. They've organized the Toyota Branch Ex–Military Fraternity and Hoei-Kai (Toyota Prosperity Club), with small branches in every shop in every plant—the best-organized fraternity in Japan. More than 470 of the 2,500 hold the rank of team chief or foreman. There are a total of 5,200 foremen and team chiefs at Toyota (3,800 team chiefs and 1,400 foremen), of which nearly 10 percent are ex–military men. This agrees with the company's policy: "From the beginning of their employment, we do not consider men discharged from the Self-Defense Forces as mere manpower. [In other words, the rest of us are considered "mere manpower."] We very much expect that they will be a leading force in our company, take the initiative, and set an example for the young workers."

The reasons ex–military enter Toyota are given in the following order: they are approached by members of the corps, by former military men already at Toyota; they read a military newspaper; they are approached by local military recruiting offices. Clearly, the Self-Defense Forces themselves are a strong influence. Ninety percent of the men enter Toyota between the ages of nineteen and twenty-five, coming straight from the regiments. Of the three forces (ground, sea, and air), as of 1971, 83.7 percent came from the Ground Force. Additionally, between 1967 and 1971, Toyota received orders for $11 million worth of military equipment. Inagaki concludes in his article that Toyota is now a growing client, a major force in the Japanese military-industrial complex.

Sunday, February 4

I rarely have time to sit and talk with the others in my team. But when we do talk over a glass of *sake*, they speak frankly of their discontent, even to a seasonal worker like me.

Worker A's story:

"Now the work is nearly three times tougher than when I came here six or seven years ago. Around 1965, they measured our work by stopwatch. Since then it's been getting tougher. But until a couple of years ago we still had enough workers, and the line used to stop ten minutes before finishing time. After the Tsutsumi plant was built in December 1970, everything really got worse. They changed from the daytime single shift to the two-consecutive-shift system, and now we've got day and night split shifts with time between shifts. And they keep speeding up the line. The faster the line gets, the harder we work to catch up, because we want to go home quickly. But when we finally get used to the speed, then they make it even faster. Right now it's a minute and fourteen seconds per unit, but I bet they'll speed it up. The new guys can't handle it any more. You read in the newspapers that Toyota workers are quick and active. We're not quick. We're forced to work quickly. It's the ones up there who benefit by exploiting us down here. I'm sure the section managers know very well how hard a time we're having. And the union, they're supported by our money, but they only work for the company. You can't expect anything from them because the leaders are all general foremen and foremen. They change every year, so nobody has enough time to get into the job seriously. If you complain to them, they just tell you to 'cooperate' and say, 'Unless you produce more your salary will not go up.'

"Two years ago we talked about ending overtime, but we realized that we couldn't make ends meet without it, so nothing changed. Personally, I enjoy physical labor. I like to work with my hands. But here, it's just too fast. I guess I can put up with the hard pace, but the trouble is I never know when I can go home. When I come home all I do is take a bath, have something to eat, and go to bed. I don't have more than an hour to talk with my wife. Nowadays I vomit whenever I'm not feeling well, and if I go see a doctor at Toyota Hospital, he just tells me to get back to work."

B's Story:

"You know Yamashita lost his finger, don't you? Or was that before you came? Anyway, during the break —we were on the second shift—the section manager came and made a speech on safety for about thirty minutes. So we were late for supper, and there were no noodles left at the canteen. We had some rice, but we all like to have a bowl of noodles at the end of the meal, you know. Afterwards we complained about this to the section manager. Then he took ten dollars out of his pocket and gave it to us. We handed it to our foreman, and he went out on his bicycle to buy some bread and ice cream. When he came back we stopped the line and sat around and ate. I was impressed. It was an amazing thing. I've decided to work for this section manager, and as long as he's here, I won't take any days off. I may be a fool, but I've never heard of anything like that happening at Toyota. Nobody would spend ten dollars out of his pocket for us. The section managers all think they have nothing to do with us.

"When I first came here the job was so tough I thought of quitting. I remember one morning I woke up and discovered I couldn't move my wrist. I wondered why I had to do work like this. And then I thought, once I've mastered the job it'll be a lot easier, and this idea kept me going. The people who stay here are the ones who have no other place to go and who like to endure pain. But in the end, we'll all be crushed by Toyota. There's hardly anyone at Toyota I can trust.

"The union? I hear they buy it off with women. I don't know if it's true or not, but I can't think of any other way. We all want to go home earlier. If you ask anybody, they'll say 'We don't want any more money, but let us go home without overtime.' When we come home late after overtime, we hardly have time to look at our wives, and they complain. That adds insult to injury. But they don't know what we go through. And I guess they'd better not find out. If they did, they'd tell us to quit. I don't want my wife to see what I'm doing here—it would make me feel even worse. I work for the sake of my children, and my only enjoyment here is having a good laugh over dumb jokes during the lunch break. Other than that, I don't have any hopes for this job.

"If you quit, Kamata, another guy'll take your place. With a new worker, the line'll stop again, and we won't be able to go home until we finish the day's quota. We'll be up shit creek."

Toyota's current slogan is "Toyota . . . Cars to Love, the World Over." On television, a charming film star, Sayuri Yoshinaga, smiles and says, "It's the car with distinction, the care for someone special." The people who buy the cars never realize that they were made, quite literally, over the dead and mutilated bodies of workers who were given no "distinction" at all.

Tuesday, February 6

On the night shift. By 5:00 A.M. I'm completely worn out. I've lost the power to think and simply move my hands absent-mindedly. Yesterday I slept only an hour during the day. I ask the others, and they all say they can't sleep during the daytime. The Monday night shift is the hardest because you can't suddenly change your sleeping and waking rhythm.

I walk home with Ogi, the "Red Line." "Hey!" I say. "You've still got thirty-nine years to go before you can retire." He answers with his usual smile, "I'll be dead before I stay here that long."

Thursday, February 8

It's a cold night. We work on the line until 7:00 A.M. After the midnight meal, Ogi says with a sigh, "Still five-and-a-half hours left. How do you guys do it?" After work the general foreman sends for me and asks, "How are you doing? Do you think you'll stay? I may arrange for you to get an extra bonus. I won't tell anyone. It's because you've worked well without taking holidays. If you can't stay for the whole month, how about two weeks? Even if we get a new worker, he'll need at least two weeks before he learns his job and can take your place. Please think about staying." Before I come back to the room, I go to the office and pick up a separation form.

Friday, February 9

It snowed last night. Ota, my fellow seasonal worker, has been absent since Monday. Miura says Ota has a bad stomach and liver and is lying in bed without eating anything. I tell him I'll go and see Ota, but he says I'd better wait. He doesn't seem to want to talk, but I gather that Ota is very depressed.

I work until 7:30 A.M. Six hours without resting. We work four-and-a-half hours before the midnight meal, so we actually put in ten-and-a-half hours. Plus thirty minutes' preparation. Today the production quota was increased by 15 to 415 boxes a day. The conveyor was speeded up to one minute and fourteen seconds per unit before we were aware of it. That's six seconds less than when I came here six months ago. Output has also increased by more than 100 boxes.

Last night as I passed the factory gate, I saw an ambulance coming out with its red light flashing. I heard that a worker had had two of his fingers crushed. There are many accidents. During the break we talk about injuries at first and end our conversation talking about stomach trouble.

"There's no one at Toyota," someone says, "who doesn't have stomach trouble." Iino and Fukuyama both tell me they were hospitalized shortly after they started at Toyota, and Ogi runs to the toilet to vomit after almost every meal. Murayama took a day off and went to see a doctor, and our team chief doesn't look well either. Lately, my stomach trouble has been getting worse, and I can't go without medicine.

Someone else says, "If you go to the Toyota Hospital, the first thing they'll ask you is if you come from the shop floor or from another section. If you say you're from the floor, then they'll tell you you don't have to be hospitalized. Just like that!"

Everyone on this line has had to have stomach X-rays with barium.

"When you take barium," someone said, "you get constipated."

"No, you don't. Not any more."

"Actually, it's colored pink and looks nice."

"My friend thought it was so good he asked for another glass!"

The extra work we'll do on Saturday is supposed to last from 8:00 P.M. to midnight, but until the last minute no one knows what time he can go home on Saturday night. Should our wives lock the door? Will we eat at home? Partly because of this uncertainty, some people want to come to work early and go home early, while others want to work the whole day since they have to come to work anyway. We are skillfully shuffled and divided, and in the end management gets what it wants.

Saturday, February 10

Overtime until 7:30 A.M. again. During the break, the foreman announces that starting next week one worker will be removed from the line, the line speed will be slightly reduced, and we will have to work three hours overtime. According to him, the management is complaining that while other workers are doing three hours overtime, we in the transmission plant aren't doing enough. The foreman opposed dropping a worker from the line, but the team chief proposed that one of the two inspectors be eliminated. To them, quantity is far more important than quality. When we were producing 600 boxes on a single daytime shift, we had two inspectors but they were constantly busy. Now, with more than 800 boxes, there will be only one inspector. "What the hell is going on?" someone asks.

The *Toyota* reports on February 9 that the annual target for "Good Idea Suggestions" is now 220,000 instead of the original target of 200,000 set last October. After they counted the number of individual targets reported by each worker at each office and plant, they increased the target by 10 percent. This leaves everyone with at least 5.5 "Good Idea Suggestions" to make.*

Sunday, February 11

Last night I stayed away from the extra Saturday work. This morning I go to the next dormitory for breakfast and see a notice on the board listing new room allotments. By April, 130 high school graduates

---

* Toyota's suggestion system was introduced in May 1951, following Ford's Rouge plant. A quota is set for each worker, and the result achieved is posted in the shop. Workers who make few suggestions are given warnings. In 1972, the total number of suggestions was 68,000 and the "participation rate" was 70 percent. A small prize is awarded—a 250-yen merchandise coupon for the co-op store, or cash to $5 usually and in rare cases to $330. Once a month a ceremony is held on the shop floor where the section manager in charge hands the rewards to the workers in envelopes that have "Good Thinking, Good Products" printed on them.

for the workshops, 120 ex-trainees (Toyota Vocational High School graduates), 190 high school graduates for clerical work, and 60 seasonal workers and probationers will move into the dorms.

After breakfast, I do some washing and pack my things so that I can leave as soon as I get my salary on the fifteenth. In the afternoon, I go to Nagoya to meet a friend. When I get back to the Toyota station, I find that the last bus has already left, although it is only eight o'clock. Since I have to return by taxi anyway, I go into a bar across from the station.

During the six months I have worked here, I've developed a very passive personality. Almost as soon as I decide to do something, I feel tired. For instance, I promised Ashino, a seasonal worker who quit soon after he arrived, that I would visit him at his new job sometime— he's working now at a pinball parlor in Nagoya. But I haven't gone to see him even once. I wanted to talk with him about Toyota, and I want to know how he's getting along, but the mere thought of going to Nagoya on a holiday and spending an hour and a half each way on the train wears me out. I think of the work that's waiting next day, and I just give up. The other day the dorm loudspeaker announced a telephone call for a seasonal worker from Hirosaki, my home town. I wrote down his room number and thought of visiting him later. But I put it off day after day, and now I feel awkward about going to see him.

When I get back in the dormitory, Hamada tells me about the dorm festival they had while I was in Nagoya. There was much drinking, and different teams put on skits. Then suddenly a drunk worker jumped onto the stage with a knife in his hand and started waving it around. Several people grabbed him and threw him out. I would like to have heard what the drunk worker had to say and what he wanted to stick his knife into. Hamada filled an empty juice bottle with *sake* and brought it back. He offers me a glass.

In the evening before he leaves for the night shift, Hamada takes a plastic bottle filled with *sake* with him to the canteen. It was originally a tea container that came with a lunch pack he received at a company-sponsored theater party for seasonal workers. He keeps a large bottle of *sake* in his closet, and pours a little at a time into the plastic bottle and drinks it before supper. He's not a heavy drinker, and says it's a custom from his farm days.

Itsuki village in Kuma County, Kumamoto Prefecture—Hamada's home town—is famous for a lullaby that goes, "After the August festival I'll be gone." Almost everyone in this poor farm town has to work as a seasonal worker in the winter. Hamada's father used to be a veterinary surgeon, but he doesn't practice any more since most of the people in the area can no longer afford to keep cattle. His family owns 3,000 square meters of rice paddies and 3,000 square meters of fields where they've begun to grow mushrooms. He says if I ever visit his town it won't be hard to find his house. "When you get off the bus, just ask any of the villagers for the Hamadas, who are always away working as seasonal workers. They'll know who you mean." He has seven brothers and sisters. He was the first son, after four daughters. Like Hamada, the next brother came to Toyota after he was discharged from the military. He lives in a dormitory near by. The third brother is also in the military and is now stationed in

Saitama Prefecture. The fourth brother is the only one who has gone to Tokyo, where he works in a printing company. The roommates of his brother at Toyota are all ex–military, and they have all regretted coming here.

"What's the military like?" I ask.

After a short pause Hamada says, "It's not bad. They feed you, give you a salary, and let you get a license." Then he adds, "The Self-Defense Forces are like a watchdog."

"A watchdog?"

"Yeah. When a house is guarded by a dog it frightens strangers. Other countries won't make fun of us if we have a watchdog."

Monday, February 12

Four more days and I'll be free! I leave the dorm a little early to see the foundry where Hamada works. The place is dark and dusty with powdered casting. I look for him through the dark workshop and find him standing on a slanting platform a little above floor level, wearing a white mask and a yellow helmet. A big conveyor belt coming up from below carries round cast pieces stuck together as if they had just come from the press. They look like branches with fruit. Hamada and another worker hit them with big hammers and separate the "fruit" from the "branches." Then, with big pincers, Hamada grasps the "branches" and throws them into a metal box. The rest is a repetition of this same action, over and over again. He has to climb onto the moving conveyor belt to do the job. Sometimes the casts are still red-hot and burn his hands. Often, they are already cold. Shortly after he came to Toyota he caught the flu. He says it was be-

153

cause of his constant exposure to extreme heat and cold. Once he came over to see me at my job and said, "It seems busy over here, but at least the temperature doesn't change. You're lucky."

The Monday morning meeting usually begins with the general foreman's speech. We gather around him and try to look solemn.

"As you already know from the newspapers, Nissan is catching up with us. But we can't let them! We can't lose! I want all of you to do your best. I understand that, tentatively, you've been asked to work on Saturdays following the night shift. I know it isn't easy, but I hope you'll cooperate. Make sure you don't take holidays without notice.

"As for your paid holidays, they are given to you by the company. Don't think that you can take holidays at your own convenience. Be sure you get permission from your boss and don't fail to give advance notice. If you take a day off, others have to suffer for it. So don't be absent.

"Ota, a seasonal worker, is now in the hospital. I hope you won't end up there too. I hope you'll take good care of yourselves, for your sake and for the sake of your team. I want you to rest enough on Sundays so you'll be able to work again on Monday."

Today a new seasonal worker arrives. He's going to take my place. His number is 8819920—he's the 1,281st worker after me. Despite all the advertisements, they haven't recruited more than 1,300 people. He's thirty-five, single, and comes from Kobe. He used to work for the Morinaga Candy Company, where he fitted lids on fruit-juice bottles. He was a temporary worker there and could be fired at any moment. On Friday last week, he worked with another shift on a trial basis and practiced the movements, but he isn't good enough yet. In the time I finish three boxes, he can't finish even one. When RY or RK models come, he has to give up. That's natural. The pace of the line is six seconds faster than when I started. From now on, no one will be able to manage it unless he's exceptionally fast, agile, and persevering.

During the break, he asks me, "How many days can most seasonal workers endure?"

"Some, well, one day; some, three days; but the majority about a week," I answer.

"Three days is more than enough for me," he says, relieved. "When I first came here, a section manager or a department manager, I'm not sure which, told me that anyone can do the job, but I'd say no one can do this." Ashino, who left to work in the pinball parlor, used to say the same thing. I myself have a feeling that I've held out till today because of some strange pride that "anyone can do the job." I don't want to fail. Naturally no one wants to fall behind. I've often heard the lifers say, with some conceit and more self-contempt, "If you can bear the work in Toyota, you can work anywhere."

The new guy stops promptly at 4:30 P.M., the regular finishing time. I guess he'll quit. I leave the shop at 6:00 P.M. They tell me they've computed my overtime hours as one-and-a-half hours a day until the day I leave. That suits me. The team chief is already working in place of Ota, who's in the hospital, and the foreman in place of Ogi, who went home at 5:00 without doing overtime. There's no one in relief to take my place. "Never mind, we'll manage somehow," says the foreman. Today the line stopped for about thirty minutes because the machine broke down and also because a new man was working on the line. I wonder how many extra hours they'll have to work tonight.

In the evening, I go to see Ota. He is on the second floor of the new four-story hospital facing our dormitory. There are six or seven people packed into the small room. He's sitting on a bed in new blue-striped pajamas, which he must have bought in a hurry when he was hospitalized, and he looks thin and pale. He seems surprised and touched to see me. "I was worn out, you know, so I started drinking again. First just one glass and then two and then three . . ." He used to joke a lot and was always in good spirits. But today he keeps grumbling; he seems changed. "Toyota is worse than the little companies. What do they think we are?" Most of the people in the room are Toyota workers. He whispers, "If you go to Toyota Hospital they won't let you stay there, so I've come to this private clinic." He says he is short of money since he just sent his salary home. He asks me over and over again to tell Miura to bring him his salary on the twentieth, payday, since his hospital fee, among other things, hasn't been paid. According to Miura, Ota has two little daughters waiting for him back in Tokushima. Ota was always a hard worker, self-confident—a real craftsman. But sitting up on that hospital bed thinking about home and the money he isn't able to send any more, he looks very gloomy. I tell him his sickness wasn't caused by alcoholism but by overwork. I also tell him that they can't fire him for getting sick (he's afraid they will), and that in case he's fired for another reason, he'll get a dismissal allowance of at least a month's salary, and that his health insurance will cover his illness even after he goes back home. His voice is full of emotion as he says, "If I'd come to Toyota on my own, I'd have quit a long time ago. But I came here with Miura, so I can't let him down." I remember that Kudo, who also got sick and went home, once told me he thought of quitting in December, but didn't because of me. The work here is so difficult that people try to support and encourage one another, especially the ones who come here together. We feel it's not fair to drop out and go home alone.

The management thinks of its regular workers as disposable parts, and even worse of its seasonal workers: seasonal workers are consumed in much shorter cycles. Even if their performance is poor, management doesn't mind as long as they can help keep the line moving for the time being. Kudo and Ota, though, got sick and the company regards them as defective merchandise to be thrown away as quickly as possible.

When I say goodbye to Ota and tell him I'm about to leave and won't be able to visit him again, he leans forward and asks me, with a desperate look, to wait for him in the toilet and slip him a few cigarettes. "I had to stop smoking all of a sudden and it's killing me." I go with him into the toilet. "I'll only give you one," I say, but I give him two. As I hand them to him I see his eyes fill with tears. Coming downstairs, I look back and see him still standing in his pajamas in the dark corridor.

Tuesday, February 13

Two probationers arrive. One is number 8534463. This is the 583rd since the probationer who had worked at Datsun arrived in October. Since my arrival, Toyota has hired about 2,000 probationers and seasonal workers. I wonder if half of them are still here.

Today, as yesterday, the line stops several times. Some machines aren't working well; a new seasonal worker is assigned to my post and a probationer is placed at the end of the line. We're all still tired from Saturday's work. However long the line stops, an equal amount of overtime will be demanded. Sugiyama and Shimoyama are upset, and Shimoyama leaves at the regular finishing time. My replacement says, "I can't stand any more," and walks away at the regular finishing time. Ogi, who's underage, leaves at 5:00 P.M., and I go at 6:00 P.M. The foreman, the team chief, and the subchief are all working on the line but they aren't enough. Even the newly arrived probationers are being asked to work at the pace of veterans.

The *Toyota Weekly* has an article on a report of grievances sent to the labor union. The workers submitted only twenty-five official grievances to the union between September and December. Only twenty-five grievances! Clearly, this shows what the workers think of the union. And what are those grievances? Eight of them are about bad meal service, seven about the bad working environment, five about insufficient company housing, and two about the lack of parking space. Most of the grievances are from the older factories.

Wednesday, February 14
Tomorrow's the last day of my contract! My replacement does not show up. I think he's had it. Murayama is absent, too. Yoshizaki has gone to a military base to recruit workers. The line moves steadily all day without any breakdowns.

Hagiwara, who works ahead of me, asks the foreman when he comes around, "How long do we have to work today?"

"Until eight," the foreman says. "Hell, I'm only joking. I want to go home early, too." When I leave the line, Hagiwara asks me if I'll be leaving at the regular time tomorrow. He's already worrying about the shortage.

Now there's only one inspector, and he's the team chief. Just as we thought, he skips quite a few boxes. Yesterday a worker acted as inspector, but he couldn't keep up and left a pile of boxes. The team chief was really mad because the section manager happened by and discovered the pile and got onto him about it. The worker was pulled off the post, and the team chief took over. As usual, production before quality!

Thursday, February 15

I wake up around five this morning and hear the clatter of empty cans echoing coldly on concrete as someone sorts them out of the trashcans. At 6:45 the sound of the morning chimes blares over the loudspeaker. Soon, I hear car engines warming up in the parking lot below my window. Then the clatter and hiss and banging of the heating system being turned on. Bright sunshine falls in through the cracks of my curtains. Fine weather. I couldn't sleep last night and stayed up until one. I was excited and nervous wondering if I could hold out one more day . . .

At the end of the morning meeting, the foreman orders me to stand beside him in the center of a circle and says, "Thank you very much for working with us for such a long time." He seems sincere. During the lunch break, as I walk to the canteen, a regular worker joins me.

"Finally finishing, aren't you?"

"Yeah, I'm getting out of this prison."

"Us regulars are condemned to life imprisonment, I guess," he says, looking at the ground.

During the break, a guy I've never had a chance to talk to comes up to me at the locker-room bench.

"You've only got three-and-a-half hours to go, haven't you? I wish I did, too. I've got to stay here for life. And no matter how hard I try, I doubt if I'll ever be able to wear a white general foreman's cap."

"Hey, you better not get too excited yet," someone else says. "I know a guy, a seasonal, who drank the night he left and went walking with a girl and got run over by a car."

"Maybe that was the best thing that could've happened," another guy says. "Better to die happy than be killed little by little in this goddamn factory."

Finally, it's time to go. Shimoyama, who works two positions ahead of me on the line, keeps coming over to tease me.

"You'll be hit by the impactor at the last second," he says.

"Only thirty minutes left!"

At 4:27 the foreman comes over to take my place. He smiles and says simply, "OK. That's all. You need time to change." Somehow, it is all too simple. I feel strange, as if resigning means simply changing places with somebody. I go around the line and say goodbye to everyone. Shimoyama holds out his hand. Takeda says with a big smile, "Thanks for everything." One worker says, "If you come back, you'd better get a softer job in one of the subcontracting companies." The line doesn't let us stop and talk. The team chief and the deputy section manager in the office look at me as if I don't exist. I go to the personnel office to get my pay and pick up some papers for unemployment insurance.

My wages for twelve days' work, including basic pay, overtime, night work, and other fringe allowances together with the final bonus of $43, come to $197.40. Net pay: $185.08. As he hands me the money the clerk says, "Mr. Kamata, you earned it." He knows how it is. "Isn't there anyone else finishing today?" I ask. "There was one in December." Only two completed their contracts at the main plant—only Yamamoto and I. Two! At first I can't believe it. After I get my money, I take a last slow walk around the place. It all seems so simple and matter-of-fact, putting an end to such hard work just like that. It isn't so much a feeling of liberation as of weariness and emptiness. I have a dull pain in my right wrist; my right fingers are stiff; my palms have shreds of metal in them; my back is sore all over; I feel continually nauseated. These are the only things I can take with me.

I return to my room and find Hamada still in bed. I show him my pay slip and tell him how to read it. He looks at it closely and says, "I'll try hard to complete my contract." I go to the dormitory office and return my key, name tag, and bedding. The clerk glances at me, but doesn't say anything, not even thank you. I'm still nothing more to them than a thing. My neighbor Miyamoto drives me to the nearest train station. As soon as I sit down I'm overcome by fatigue, cold, and a deep desire to sleep.

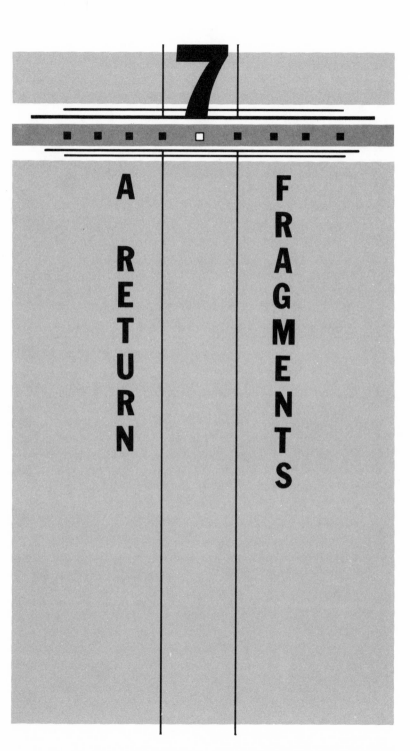

7

A RETURN

FRAGMENTS

Tuesday, March 28

In Hirosaki, it's snowing. I walk around looking for Kudo's house. It begins to snow harder, and I feel the flakes in my hair. I start coughing and take a cough drop. The road is winding, but I meet a high school boy who tells me the way. Still, I miss Kudo's house and have to ask the way again. It's a tiny house, hidden from the road and very quiet.

His mother, a plump woman, opens the door. She has something in her mouth; she must have been eating a late breakfast. Soon Kudo appears. He looks very pale, but somehow serene, almost a different person. I realize now how unnatural he looked while we were living together, how exhausted he had been. He comes out into the small entranceway. His mother follows him with his coat and puts it over his shoulders. "Shall we go out?" he says. He wants to be alone while he talks with me. "He just got out of bed," his mother cuts in apologetically, "and we have to go to the hospital soon." I learn that his mother goes with him even to the hospital, which is only twenty minutes away. He's been sick in bed ever since he came back from Toyota.

He looks at his mother and repeats his catchphrase: "I was lucky." Then he tells his mother, "He's also from Hirosaki." "Thank you very much," his mother says, "for everything you've done for him." "Damn tough job!" he says in the accent he picked up at Toyota. I'm afraid that it might weaken him to talk any longer, so I close the door myself and leave. It's snowing even harder.

Monday, April 9

In Tokushima, I get out of the taxi and find myself in a dusty spot in the midst of tiny houses, apartments, and small factories. It reminds me of the outskirts of Tokyo, where small workshops stand next to rice paddies. Radio and television antennas rise here and there, high into the air. I last saw Ota when I visited him in the hospital. Now he lives in one of the small semi-detached houses behind a concrete company apartment. No one is home, and the front door is locked with a padlock. The nextdoor neighbor tells me that his parents and a younger brother who is still in school live there, though they're all out today. The neighbor suddenly remembers that his married younger sister lives near by.

After five or six minutes' walk I come to a small house facing a rice paddy. A young woman stands in front with a baby in her arms. It's Ota's younger sister. Her nose is exactly the same. "We haven't heard from him at all," she says, worried. She also tells me that sometime in March they received a telegram from the Toyota Motor Company asking if he'd returned. After leaving the hospital, he had told someone that he would go to Nagoya for a few days, and since then, he hadn't come back to the factory or the dormitory. Nobody had heard from him. His family only found out that he'd been in the hospital because he wrote to ask them to send back the money he'd sent them. I remember he told me when I visited him in the hospital that he didn't want his family to know about it. He must be hard up.

It puzzles me that the address he'd given me was his parents', despite his being married, and that his married sister knew everything about him. "Where is his family?" I ask. After a slight hesitation, his sister says, "They've gone back to her parents."

Friday, April 20

In a coffee shop in Toyota, reading the *Chunichi Daily*, I find this: "At Toyota a truck ran wild. The steering broke and it went out of control!"

I read on:

On April 19, around 11:45 A.M., on Route 248 in Toyota City, a Toyota DA20 truck driven by S. Kato (twenty years old) of a forwarding company crossed the dividing line and struck a car in the opposite lane. The truck then smashed through a cement-block fence, hit a car parked in a neighboring vacant lot, and finally crashed to a stop against the wall of a bedding shop. The car parked in the vacant lot was badly damaged, and the shop had a part of its wall destroyed, but fortunately there was no one near and no casualties. The driver was not seriously injured. The accident occurred only 550 yards from the Main Plant of the Toyota Motor Company, where the truck was made. The truck was being sent to the Kamigo plant of the Toyota Motor Sales Company, and had not been mounted with a bed platform. The police are now investigating. The driver said he was about to turn a curve when the truck's steering wheel suddenly went out. He didn't have time to step on the brakes. Investigators found that some of the bolts that connect the steering shaft to the front-wheel gear box were missing. This disconnected the steering,

167

and the truck went out of control. They found marks the bolts had made, however, so the police think that bolts weren't fastened properly and came off as the truck jolted. The police are now questioning the person in charge of the plant. The Toyota Motor Company is also making an independent investigation.

This accident is a direct result of the Toyota policy that places production before safety. I vividly remember the workers who were rushed by the conveyor lines.

Sometime after eight o'clock last night I called up my old dormitory. Hamada was still there. When I said who I was, he was really surprised. We arranged to meet at a coffee shop in front of the dorm. I hurried there by taxi and found him waiting for me outside. "I thought you were calling all the way from Aomori!" he said with his usual friendly smile. After having some beer at a stall near the dorm, we went to his room. The pinups Kudo had put up on the wall were still there. Miyamoto, who'd been in the next room, had moved to another dorm, and there were now two seasonal workers there from Okinawa, who were assigned to the assembly line at the Main Plant. In Hamada's workshop there's also a worker from Okinawa. I remembered something I once heard on the bus coming back from a company-sponsored theater party in Nagoya. A man from the Personnel Department was telling his friend that he was about to go to Okinawa to recruit workers. He said the transportation cost $230 but that he had to go since Nissan had recruited many workers in Okinawa, and so on.

The worker who moved in with Hamada after me is thirty-five, a single guy from Kumamoto. He told Hamada that he had worked as a painter, but Hamada thinks he's a "drifter." He was on the night shift and wasn't in the room. His bed wasn't made, and the bed was surrounded by empty cheap whisky bottles and empty milk bottles, plus a November 1970 issue of the Japanese edition of *Reader's Digest*. Hamada laughed and said he'd never seen this guy wash his things or clean his room. The guy works at an electric furnace in a foundry. He had an accident soon after he started working. A red-hot ingot slipped into his glove and badly burned his right thumb. This injury, however, was not considered worthy of coverage by Workers' Compensation Insurance. He took three days off and went to work the following Monday, and they act as if nothing happened.

Hamada took a photo out of the pocket of his jacket. It showed his wife, a boy who has just entered grade school, and a little girl, all sitting on the grass smiling. He said it was taken on a picnic. "They're tall for their ages, aren't they?" I said, and he answered proudly, "I don't know why. My wife and I aren't tall, but they're quite tall." On the twenty-fifth he'll complete his contract. He's already sent his luggage home, including some souvenirs for his family. On the morning of the twenty-sixth he'll finish working. He's already imagining how he'll come back to the dorm for the last time, pack up whatever he has left, and say good-bye to his brother in the next dorm. Then he'll take an express train, which will get him home by the evening of the following day. I guess this is the most uneasy period for him.

Saturday, April 21
This morning Hamada sees me off at the bus stop. On a sidewalk by the gate, we notice a man of over fifty sitting, resting his back against the fence with his work

shoes beside him. "Going to your side job today?" Hamada asks. The man doesn't reply. Hamada raises his voice and asks again. The elderly man opens his eyes a little, recognizes Hamada, and nods slightly. "He's really tough!" Hamada says. He tells me that not a few seasonal workers do side jobs over the weekend. Hamada himself used to work with this man; they worked in one of the subcontracting factories for the Tsutsumi plant. Hamada worked as an assistant to a regular worker, supporting a ladder while the worker repaired ventilation pipes and handing him tools. "It was easy work, and they paid me nine dollars and thirty cents a day. I almost felt guilty," he says. He knew that if Toyota found out he'd be in trouble, but he wore his Toyota jacket there anyway.

Many regular workers also have side jobs. Since the company doesn't allow them to live in its housing for more than ten years, they're forced to buy their own houses. At the end of March, a team chief at one of the Toyota plants was killed in an accident while he was working as a ditchdigger. Another worker told me that he worked for a car delivery firm. He drove cars one way, but the company didn't provide him with return fare. Not many conveyor-line workers have the time and energy to do side jobs.

Sunday, April 22

Rain. I wanted to see Takeda, another fellow I used to work with. I wonder what's happened to him. We used to walk home together after work, and he'd say, "I guess I'd better make up my mind and quit." I turn the corner and follow the path we used to take, and eventually come to a block of apartment houses rented mainly to Toyota workers. His name is on the list at the gate. I knock at his door, but no answer. I turn the knob and the door opens. The small entrance is filled with three or four pairs of mountaineering boots. I walk in and find him sleeping on the floor, taking up most of the room. He seems to have fallen asleep as soon as he came back from the night shift. I shake him slightly, and he opens his eyes, shuts them again, and then springs up, surprised.

After waking up, he says, "I'm going to quit after I get my summer bonus." He wanted to quit in April and enter a professional cooking school in Kyoto, but he sent in the papers too late, so he decided to wait until the summer bonus. I tell him there are cooking schools in Tokyo, too, but he says, as he always does, that he doesn't like Tokyo. Ho begins telling me about his dream: he wants to learn Western cooking and to open his own restaurant. He'll inherit a small piece of land near Shizuoka, and if he sells it he may be able to raise enough money to realize his dream.

The walls are covered with photos of mountains, and there are some books on mountaineering on a small bookshelf. Looking at the photos, I imagine him standing behind his restaurant counter wearing a billowing white apron and a cook's cap. He's not a talkative person, but if he marries a sociable wife, together they'll be a success.

Only the Toyota Personnel Department has the exact figures on how many workers quit in despair, but there is a way to estimate it. In the spring of 1972, Toyota employed 3,200 school graduates (*Toyota*, November 24, 1972). As of November 1971, Toyota had 40,918 employees (*Financial Statement*). In November 1972, the number of employees was 41,256. Despite the addition of 3,200 school graduates, the net increase was only 338. This means that about 3,000 workers quit. Besides, every year at odd times they hire, according to the union, 3,000 probationers who aren't regular employees. Of these, 500 are made regular employees, according to the Public Relations Department. In other words, 2,500 of them quit in a year. Furthermore, the company hires nearly 2,000 seasonal workers a year. In my workshop, only 30 percent finished their contracts. If the average ratio of those who finish is slightly above 50 percent for all plants, this means 1,000 more workers quit. This adds up to about 7,000 workers who give up on Toyota every year. Also, many of the trainees drop out halfway through.

The present Toyota production and labor management systems are literally liquidating just under 7,000 workers a year. Toyota workers often tell stories of people who kill themselves by jumping off dormitory roofs or off the tops of machines. The workers say these incidents are never reported in the papers. I read that in 1965 there were ten suicides and forty psychiatric cases.[*]

The Personnel Department has taken some formal measures aimed at "motivating" workers and increasing their morale: it has instituted a system whereby workers indicate which jobs they would like to work at, a new ranking system, and a rotation system for workers, and it stresses the development of individual ability (*Toyota*, November 24, 1972). Yet this re-

---

[*] Research Association for the Analysis of Monopoly, *Monopoly in Japan*, vol. 3 (Tokyo: Shin Nippon Publishing Co., 1970).

organization of control initiated by the management does not alter the workers' basic feelings of alienation.

The labor union, on the other hand, has given up dealing with the problems in the plant, and chants phrases such as "restoration of life" through an "increase in leisure hours." The workers put very little faith in the present labor union.

The April 1973 issue of the *Toyota Union Monthly* has a report on the United States' automobile industry by a union official. He writes that in General Motors' Lordstown plant, famous as the site of the "robots' revolt," 2,000 grievances were presented, while in the St. Louis plant 12,000 grievances were submitted by its 11,000 union members. Yet he writes, "I honestly think the auto workers in Japan are working a lot more than their American counterparts."

Monday, April 23

I go with another worker to visit Kisaburo Onoe. He's now working at Toyota and has been fighting for recognition of his occupational disease for the past four years. He's not a typical "activist." I find him sick in bed with a foot warmer in a small rented room. He talks slowly and wearily, and when I ask him to draw a map of the workshop where he used to work, his hand trembles as he draws the lines. His writing is almost illegible. But as he talks, his voice becomes strong with anger, and sometimes he speaks humorously.

He came to work at Toyota in May 1967, when he was thirty-five. He was sent to the stamping shop at the Motomachi plant. He had left an affiliated firm, Toyota Auto Body Company, and joined the parent firm because it was more conveniently located. During the year and three months until he was made a regular worker, his job was to lift pressed roofs from the conveyor line with another worker, walk backwards carrying them, and stack them on top of each other. A Crown or Corona roof weighs about thirty-five pounds —and he had to carry 260 of them an hour. From morning to night, he kept on repeating this: lifting a thirty-five-pound roof, walking backwards with it, and then stacking it.

Onoe was the only one who lasted a year. One of the three others was frequently absent without notice, another got transferred, and the third quit.

A month before he was promoted to regular worker, he was assigned to making roofs, using a press. There was no particular skill involved, and there wasn't anyone else available at the time. It was much easier than the job he was doing before. He was in charge of the second press. There had been two workers who carried roofs from the first to the second press, but they were replaced by an automatic crane. The crane lifted a roof from the first press and put it on the conveyor line in front of him. He then put it in place and pressed it with his machine. "Dangerous as hell to stand close to," he says. "The roofs came dropping right down! Swinging from side to side! Only men can do that job. Machines can't do it." Onoe was well-built and stronger than the others, and he pressed nearly 260 roofs in an hour, and 2,500 a day. He could finish 250 more than any other worker, which made him proud.

Then, on May 9, 1969, it happened. There had been something wrong with his machine since the night before. He was ordered to operate it slowly since it caused distortions at high speeds. But because the automatic crane was working at its normal high speed,

174

three roofs arrived on the conveyor for every one he could handle. He had to hold the other two with his right hand and press the first one very quickly in order to keep up. At around 3:40 P.M., after six hours straining to hold metal roofs that weighed thirty-five pounds and standing in a strained position, he felt a sharp pain shoot from the right side of his back and shoulder up to the back of his head. The pain was so bad he couldn't stand up.

He went to work the next day and the following three days, even though he couldn't move his right arm (at Toyota you're supposed to come to work even if you're injured), and did light jobs such as cleaning the floor. On the night of May 13 he was assigned to work at a machine that pressed Corona hoods, which were slightly smaller than roofs. But his right arm and shoulder were still very painful, and he felt he couldn't do the job. He asked the foreman to take him off the line, but the foreman said, "I don't give a damn how much you itch or ache. It's not my business." Onoe left the workshop earlier than usual. That night he went to see a nearby dentist, and, although it was eleven o'clock at night, he had a molar extracted. He thought his headache was caused by a decayed tooth. At first, the dentist refused to pull it, saying it wasn't bad, but Onoe insisted. "You have to take a day off to go to the dentist or else you have to line up at three in the morning. If you've waited that long, you'll ask the dentist to pull all your bad teeth at one shot," he says. Although there are 200,000 people in Toyota City, there are not enough dentists or doctors.

His headache didn't get any better, and his right arm remained numb. He stayed home a few more days, but he soon went back and continued to work with his left hand until the end of May. Since his injury was obviously occupational, he asked the general foreman to give him written recognition, but the general foreman (according to him) said, "If you keep this up I'll fire you." A safety campaign called "Five Million Safe Hours" was under way, and the general foremen and foremen were doing everything they could to hide accidents in their own workshops. Company regulations require occupational accidents to be reported in three days, so his case was thrown out. He took two weeks sick leave at the end of May, and when the foreman "advised" him to present a medical certificate of any sort or be fired, he submitted a certificate saying he had "neuralgia." The company is now using this as a proof that he has neuralgia and not an occupational injury.

His headache persisted while he was on leave, and he couldn't sleep. "I couldn't hold chopsticks or tolerate the breeze from an electric fan or even a slight wind outside," he said. He returned to work, but after a few days he decided to go back home to Sendai and recuperate. He received regular treatment there, but he didn't improve. Finally he visited the local Labor Standards Inspection Office, which advised him to formally request recognition of his occupational accident. In December 1969 he got a certificate from the medical department of Nagoya University that said he showed "specific upper arm and shoulder symptoms caused by his occupation." He submitted this certificate along with his request to the Labor Standards Inspection Office in Okazaki, where Toyota is located.

The company, however, prevented Onoe's colleagues from testifying about him. "Tell them you don't remember anything about Onoe," the management ordered. "Tell them that the second press never has been operated at reduced speed." The inspectors who came listened to the company's explanation and left. The materials they employed were very biased toward the company, even using a picture of a newly installed automatic press that had been put in just after the accident.

In March 1971, the Okazaki Labor Standards Inspection Office decided, "Although we admit that the work put a fairly heavy burden on his arm, we cannot consider it 'exceptionally severe use of hands and fingers' or 'very vigorous work.' Therefore we do not recognize the illness as being occupational in nature."

The union's attitude was typified by the union president, who said, "I don't know anything about it. Go and talk to the director of the union welfare department." The director said, "We can't say anything once the management has made a decision."

After a year and seven months, Onoe went back to work in January 1971. Out of more than twenty colleagues, he only found four or five still remaining; the rest had all left. Before his injury, he used to get out a chessboard during the lunch break and play, whistling cheerfully. But after his illness, he couldn't concentrate on the game any more. Worse, the other workers avoided him. If they saw a boss coming, they suddenly disappeared. Apparently the company had spread a rumor that Onoe's friends were "reds." People wondered why somebody with a physique like his was doing cleaning and other minor jobs. Tormented by headaches and his numb arm, unable to work properly, refused recognition of his occupational illness, he thought of committing suicide many times. He even burned his diary and papers.

In May 1971, he appealed to the Workmen's Accident Compensation Insurance Council. He's been waiting for two years, but no decision has yet been made. Despite all this, he is no activist but an ordinary hard-working laborer who goes to work every day. "I wish the workers at Toyota would support me a little more," he says. " 'We hope you win,' they tell me, but that's all." He tells me that the thing that keeps him going is the thought of the many workers who left Toyota quietly without demanding recognition of their occupational illness. He's determined to win. "I can't seem to give up. Maybe I'm a fool . . ." he says, smiling quietly.

Tuesday, April 24

I meet a worker from my old workshop. "Back to see us?" he says. "Got a new job?" He talks of the changes. Before I left, a thirty-five-year-old seasonal worker from Kobe was assigned to take my place, but he soon quit and the subchief took over. Then a twenty-year-old seasonal worker from Hokkaido came, but he also left. Finally, another young man came from Kyushu. At the time, Toyota was (as always) short of hands, and there was no one in relief. Around 10:00 A.M. they stopped the line for a five-minute "toilet break," during which this new worker went out to the locker room and never came back. After this they had another seasonal worker from Kyushu, but today he didn't show up. A regular worker has been sent in, and he may stay.

I'm not surprised. When I started working, the line moved six seconds per piece slower than it does now, and it took me nearly two months to get used to the job. The two probationers who came in before I left have already quit. Like bodies dropping on a battle-field! Since there's no resistance in the workshop, the remaining regular workers have to make up the difference. Starting next month, the final assembly line will go on a two-shift system, too. The target: 1,000 boxes a day. That's 250 boxes, or 25 percent more, than what it was when I first came here!

Wednesday, April 25

Many of the young workers who quit Toyota say, "I've become normal since I left the company." Daté is one of them, though with his outgoing personality he still has many friends among the Toyota workers. We arrange to meet a worker friend of his at a coffee shop. He arrives with a handsome, long-haired young guy wearing a blue-jeans suit.

The man entered Toyota two years ago through a personal introduction. He graduated from night high school and worked at a small factory during the day. The first thing he says is "I'd like to speak honestly about the company. I'm a little eccentric." But before we've been talking five minutes, he starts looking around uncomfortably and says, "I wonder if it's OK to talk like this?" We decide to go to a bar near by, but there too he looks around every time a customer walks in. Finally he asks Daté about me: "Are you sure he's not spying on us for the company?" He asks for my business card.

This young man works at a technical job, not on the line. He calls his job stupid but not tough. He isn't satisfied with Toyota, but thinks he won't be able to earn more anywhere else. He knows very well from experience that the smaller companies are even worse than Toyota. Yet he shows a sense of superiority over the workers who came from the Toyota Vocational High School when he says, "They don't know anything. Poor bastards! They can't even quit if they're not satisfied."

Daté came from the Toyota Vocational High School, and he keeps saying, "The people who stay at Toyota are idiots!" The young man watches him without saying anything. From the way Daté talks, it's clear that he still feels a lot of friendship toward the workers at Toyota and simply wishes them a better life. After he quit Toyota, Daté supported himself as a ditchdigger and as a worker in various firms so small they could hardly be called companies. One of his friends also quit and works as a day laborer. The management call them "dropouts," and they call the remaining workers "idiots." Between the two stands Toyota, which continues to grow and racked up the highest profit in Japan last year.

The young man says, "Toyota is crafty. They know everything and always act in advance. We always find ourselves trapped."

The young man stands and walks off to the bathroom. When he comes back he suddenly says, "I learned in school about modern history, but here at Toyota we're still back in the feudal period."

Daté and I agree that the Toyota system is just like the irresponsible hierarchy of the emperor system. The team chief says, "I'm simply passing on the orders from my superiors." Then the foreman says, "My orders are the orders of my superiors." The general foreman and the section manager all say the same thing, and the workers give up resisting forced "rationalization."

A few days ago Daté introduced me to a young girl

who worked in an office for seven years after leaving high school, but who now says it's uncomfortable to continue working for Toyota. If she gets married she'll have to quit. Although it's not written anywhere in the regulations, she says every married woman leaves. It's an unwritten law. This is such common knowledge that high school teachers coach their female students not to raise their hands if they are asked at the Toyota interview whether they want to continue working after they marry. The average age of female employees at Toyota is twenty-one years and four months, which means that most girls leave three years after they graduate from high school.

In *Our Twenty-Year History*, put out by the Toyota union, there is an article about this:

The management asked the married female workers to try to understand the company's "intention" and make way for their juniors: "A number of you employees have asked us to employ female workers, but it has been impossible to meet all the demands due to the limited number of vacancies. So we want you to make way for the young, because we think it's impossible for a woman to fulfill both occupational and domestic duties."

The union strongly opposed this action in a subcommittee, but since the question was very delicate we decided that there could be no general solution. During negotiations we expressed the demands of the general members and those who are directly concerned. As a result we succeeded in getting the women a special "farewell bonus."

This article was written in 1957. Nothing seems to have changed since then.

Thursday, April 26

Daté takes me to see Enomoto. He joined Toyota in 1966 and worked for two years before being promoted to regular worker. In the engine shop at the Motomachi plant where he first worked, one group consisted of twenty-nine workers and five supervisors; during the year, a total of thirty-five workers quit. He says that at the engine assembly shop at the Kamigo plant, two lines produce one Corolla engine every thirty-five seconds and one Celica engine every twenty-nine seconds. In order to reach the daily target, the lines are operated throughout the lunch break, except for a fifteen-minute break when production is done by supervisors and others.

At first I can't believe it. He smiles and says, "Nobody believes it until they see it. Somebody wrote 'The Murderer Assembly Line' on the toilet wall."

"Don't they complain?" I ask.

"No," he says. "They don't say anything."

The day shift works from eight in the morning until eight at night, and the night shift from eight at night to eight in the morning. Only two shifts for the full twenty-four hours. The company eliminated an entire shift! The section managers compete with each other to make better records and get promoted; the general foremen, foremen, and team chiefs compete to reach the production targets and push down costs. To be promoted to supervisor, they have to give up holidays, make no complaints, and avoid "suspicious activities." They must submit as many "good ideas" as possible. If they attend meetings or activities outside the company, they're blacklisted by the Toyota security force. Workers are under constant surveillance.

Most shop stewards are chosen from among the

foremen, team chiefs, or subchiefs, and the head shop steward comes from among the general foremen. Members of the council, which is the second highest decision-making organ after the general assembly, should in principle be elected. Actually, they're appointed from among the supervisory positions, and if anyone attempts to run for a post, he's put under strong pressure to give up. The person who has the greatest power in the workshop and who manages the workers on a day-to-day basis—the general foreman —is also the union representative from the shop floor. The majority of the executive members of the Toyota Auto Workers' Union are said to be either general foremen or chief clerks (college graduates).

An election for chairman of the union executive committee was held in September 1971. For the first time in several years there was an opposition candidate, and he came from a very different background from all the executive members of the past. As expected, he lost the election. The next spring, however, the union revised its election regulations. Until then, candidates for the three chief executive posts were required to have one member who would take "responsibility" for their election campaigns. Under the new rules, more than fifty backers were required. And candidates for the executive committee need fifteen supporting signatures from one plant. This was a direct attempt to limit candidacy: as it stands now, you can't run for chief executive unless you find fifty supporters who have the courage to openly oppose the union, which emphasizes cooperation with the management. As Enomoto says, "The management is really crafty. They work us hard during every waking hour so we have no time to think of 'evil things.'

Actually, we don't have spare time for *anything*! The union plays along because it's made up of supervisors out to increase their own power. What a setup!"

Friday, April 27

I meet Mr. Natori, who ran unsuccessfully for executive chairman of the union. He's no activist. He simply ran for the position out of a personal sense of justice. He lives in a small, barely furnished one-room apartment. He says he felt very angry about the union, so he went to the election committee and asked them how he could become a candidate. He wasn't well known in the union, and he knew very little about labor unions. He didn't belong to any organization and hardly carried out an election campaign.

Still, he got 6,359 votes against the incumbent president Shiro Umemura, who got 23,900. About 5,000 nonconfidence votes were cast against the vice-president and the chief secretary, and the same number can be assumed to have been cast against Umemura. This leaves about 1,000 votes out of Natori's 6,000 that might have been cast in support of his courage.

"I have a feeling," he said, "that there were more than that."

Natori was told that ballot counting would begin at midnight on election day, so he went to the union office with his friend and asked to witness the counting. The union officers refused, saying, "You don't trust us, huh?" He was never able to witness the tabulation. According to him, the voting itself had also been supervised by the hierarchy: the workers had to fill out their ballots in front of the election committee—all of them shop supervisors.

Natori has been working for Toyota for seven years. He joined Toyota in 1966 at twenty-five. He should be promoted to team chief soon, but after he became a candidate—despite the fact that he didn't miss a single workday and had never come late to work—he was given the lowest possible evaluation. He now works on the line in the Motomachi plant, where he produces Corona Mark IIs. "There are still after-effects for me," he says. He doesn't say if he will keep on fighting. At the end of our conversation, he glances at a sparsely filled bookshelf and says, "I've been reading children's stories lately. It was only because the dog, the monkey, and the pheasant agreed to serve Momotaro* that he gave them sweet dumplings. If they hadn't followed Momotaro's orders, they wouldn't have gotten anything, would they?"

Thursday, May 3

Constitution Memorial Day. A national holiday, but at Toyota it's a normal workday. I walk about for a while in front of the gate of the Main Plant. As I'm getting on my bicycle, someone calls me from behind: "Hey! You took a photo, didn't you?" I turn around and see a plump guard of about fifty staring at the camera hanging from my shoulder. I answer, "Are you saying it's illegal to carry a camera here?" "No, no, I don't mean that, but it's like a big private house here. No one can walk about freely, you know."

I've been walking between the central canteen and the labor union building, an area that is not inside the factory premises. "Where are you going?" he asks. "I'm going to the union."

---

* Momotaro is a figure in Japanese folklore.

185

"Then I'll go with you."

"You're coming with me to the union?" I say as I start to push the bicycle I've borrowed. He looks at the name painted on the rear mudguard and says, "So you're the one who's always going to Nomimachi for a drink." He seems quite well informed. The owner of the bicycle is already on his suspected list.

Together, we go in the back entrance of the labor union building. When I step away from him to throw a cigarette butt into an ashtray, he tenses to prevent me from running away. "What are you going to do at the union?"

"That's my business."

"Whom are you going to meet?"

"I want to meet the president."

"Do you have an appointment?"

"If he is not in, I'll talk to the chief secretary or someone else."

It's lunch hour, and the union office is empty. The guard doesn't know what to do with me. From the rear end of the room, a tall man of over forty comes over, holding a sandwich in a plastic bag. "He's the vice-president," the guard says, relieved. He stares at me, observing my reaction.

When the guard has left, I talk with the vice-president, Mr. Ishikawa, who also looks at me suspiciously. He talks about the monotony and the intensity of labor. "There's not much we can do about the labor environment. We think it's important to harmonize labor and leisure, and we're trying to increase leisure time through a five-day-week system. We're also trying to rotate the workers on the line after a certain period. We're going to set up a committee for leisure planning and hold a Toyota Jamboree and other get-togethers for young people." When I ask him why so many workers quit, he answers, "They say the work is tough. We tell them we can transfer them to easier jobs, but they still quit." When I ask him about the 1950 Toyota strike, he says, "We don't think of the labor-management relation as a class confrontation. We like to think of it as a human relation. The power of a union isn't measured by its ability to strike. A union should be judged by the working conditions it gains." I ask him how many company supervisors are union officials, and he replies, "I don't want to answer."

There are hurried knocks on the door, and a uniformed security officer in his forties comes into the room. He sits down next to the vice-president and stares at me without reserve. I recall seeing him when I first came here eight months ago as a seasonal worker. He lectured us on "Traffic Manners and Security" during orientation. I didn't notice anything particular about him at the time, but now we sit facing each other. He asks me bluntly, "Where did you come from?"

"Why do you have to ask me like that?" I say.

"I hear you've been seen in the canteen, too," he continues, looking repeatedly at me and the business card I've placed in front of the vice-president.

"I came from over there," I reply, "by bicycle."

"By bicycle?" He looks surprised. I'm surprised, too, at how fast the information spreads. Somebody reported a "suspicious man" walking in and out of the canteen and told the guard who'd challenged me a few minutes before. He must have called his superior or a security officer. He tells me, "This is private property like a big house. People aren't allowed to walk around freely." I reply that I don't see why I'm not allowed to walk on the road. I tell the vice-president that a union building is supposed to be independent from the company. Even though the building is located on company premises, it has free access and freedom from restrictions by the company, even during strikes. The vice-president looks stunned: "Strikes! Our union? We never thought of . . ."

The security officer, also a union member, says, "Our union is a good union, you know." The vice-president adds, "Though outsiders make some criticisms." They look at each other and laugh. The security officer says, "I was in the May Day procession the other day and was enjoying the hustle and bustle, when I heard someone yell at us, 'You're a second LDP!'* I wonder if he was from around here." He stares at me as he says this. Soon I say goodbye and stand up to go. They also rise and walk toward the exit. As I'm walking out, the vice-president says, "There you are," and hands my business card to the security officer.

A few days later there is an anonymous phone call to my home in Tokyo. "Is Mr. Kamata doing research on traffic-accident orphans?" the man on the phone asks. But my family refuses to talk, so he hangs up. Also about that time, a city councilman I know tells Mr. Kachi, another city councilman from the Toyota Motor Company,† "A reporter from Tokyo wants to

---

* The Liberal Democratic Party is the conservative party that has ruled Japan since the Occupation.
† Currently, the mayor of Toyota City, the chairman of the City Assembly, and seven Assembly members are from Toyota or an affiliated firm.

see you." Mr. Kachi immediately replies, "He must be from Hibariga-Oka" (the area where I live in Tokyo).

One worker told me that less than five minutes after he started handing out leaflets at a single workers' dorm, the loudspeaker began warning the dormitory residents not to touch the leaflets. In a couple more minutes he was "arrested" by the dorm officers and forcibly taken to a room next to the dorm office. One of his friends who had been with him ran into the room and said, "What are you doing here? Your mother's about to die!" Before the guards had time to think, he pulled the worker into his car and drove away.

Another worker told me that while he was handing out leaflets near the main gate of the plant, he was attacked by the guards. Someone must have called the police, since a police car came and took him to the Toyota City police station.

Someone told me that the road that goes by the main gate where the guard challenged me used to be the path to a small village near by. When Toyota decided to use the road, they agreed that a lane would be left free for the villagers to use. After the 1950 strike, however, concrete posts were put up along the road with the name of the company on them, and guards started checking everyone going into and out of the dormitories and company housing.

Saturday, May 5

It's Children's Day, a national holiday. But at Toyota, as usual, it's a workday. I'd applied to the Public Relations Department for a tour through the plant, and they arranged it for today. At 10:00 A.M. I go to Toyota Hall, which is next to the main building. Last year 230,000 people took the tour.

First we see a publicity film: cars shining brilliantly in the sunlight driving down highways, along beaches, through mountains. Beautiful! We see engines being automatically grated on a transfer machine, brightly colored cars being assembled in a well-lighted factory. A narrator says, "Respect for human beings. This is the spirit of Toyota." Such a flimsy lie. All my pale, sick friends, all the seasonal workers who quit in exhaustion, where have they all gone? Kudo and Yamamoto, who worked among the old machines, dust, noise, and cold, the tense faces of the conveyor-line workers: they've all disappeared from the film.

Then I'm taken, along with a young man from Fukushima, to the Motomachi plant. Our guide is a young girl with a healthy smile. Visitors are expected to provide their own transportation, and since I don't have a car, the guide and I ride with the young man in his brand new Toyota Corolla. He says his older brother is working for Toyota.

The Motomachi plant is where Miura and I came to visit in February. I notice there are now more seasonal workers with their double-green-striped caps. The Crown assembly line has stopped and a sign saying "No Chassises" has been put up. Young seasonal workers are sweeping the floor at a leisurely pace. I feel like waving my hand to them and saying hello.

Then we visit a stamping shop. They tell me there are two hundred presses here. The presses near the line close to the visitors' observation course have one worker for each machine. A worker places a steel plate on top of the mold, moves back from the machine, and presses a button with both hands. The pressed steel plate moves automatically onto the conveyor line in front. Then he puts another steel plate onto the mold. When he presses the button, the press comes down . . . another plate . . . the same action. Is he a living press worker?

On the far side there is a fully automated conveyor line. There isn't a single worker. Instead, electro-magnets pull the steel plates and put them onto the molds. An automatic line and a human line work side by side doing the same job. It isn't machines that are copying human beings, but the human beings that are being substituted for machines. And they have to com-pete against each other to produce. Each man is beaten down and his pride broken into pieces.

I remember the publicity film. It spoke of Toyota's "respect for human beings." But there was not a single human worker in any scene. All we could see were cars and machines.

8

THE DARK SIDE

OF TOYOTA

THE WONDERLAND

Toyota Hall stands near the Toyota Motor Company's Head Office Building in an area where the hills were once covered with red pines. Now everything is different. Even the place names have been changed to honor the Toyota family, and it has become the keep of their "castle town." The two-story hall itself was built in November 1977 to commemorate the company's fortieth anniversary. It's an enormous Toyota showcase.

I arrived yesterday, January 7, 1980, the first working day of Toyota's new year. Today, however, since I don't have any appointments with workers or any other plans, I decided to pay my first visit to this showy hall—not so very different from a penny arcade. A big sign in the hall showing "The Number of Toyotas Produced up to the Present" lights up quite impressively. Its electronic panel displays a long row of figures: 29,894,140. Twenty-nine million eight hundred ninety-four thousand one hundred and forty Toyotas! This is the total number of vehicles produced since Toyota shipped out its first trial automobile in May 1935. Of course, this figure is only as of 11:15 A.M. As I watch, the last digit continually increases.

---

* This chapter was previously published in *Sekai* [The world], March 1980.

Timing it, I realize that the number is changing every six seconds. Two weeks from now, the 30 millionth car will be recorded. The 20 millionth came in July 1976. According to the guide, this figure includes all the cars and trucks finished at the five Toyota plants as well as Toyota Chassis, Arakawa Chassis, Hino, and Daihatsu—Toyota-affiliated firms. One new vehicle every six seconds!

The computer in the control room, which occupies one corner of the Head Office Building, assesses the rate of production through circuits linking the various plants, and quickly computes the number on the panel. It is the perfect symbol of mass production. Standing in front of it, an executive would probably nod in satisfaction—or would he feel impatient seeing that the six seconds have not yet been reduced to five?

Watching the figure increase with each passing second, I feel all choked up. I can see it: the conveyor belts moving along mercilessly; the workers moving frantically as they try to keep up. I can hear their sighs. One vehicle every six seconds. The conveyor belts never stop. Workers are already dead tired. Figures racking up on the panel without a break. For a few moments, I just stand there stunned.

The wind carries shouts from the adjacent athletic field. Preparations are under way for the New Year's Parade of Security Division Fire Brigades, which is scheduled for the afternoon. In the empty Exhibition Hall (where the first visitors of the year have not yet appeared), part-time women workers are polishing cars. The 1980 auto-production competition is just about to start.

Yesterday, the president's annual New Year's address was delivered in this hall's big auditorium. Eiji

Toyota spoke to his seven hundred middle- and top-management employees: "We already depend on overseas markets for about one-half of our products. Overseas markets are extremely important. I ask you to see things from a broad international point of view, and I also want you to carry out your daily work always keeping in mind the overseas situation."

Last year's sales of Japanese automobiles (Toyotas, Datsuns, and others) in the United States reached 1,770,000, a 30.5 percent increase over the previous year. Both General Motors and Ford have been preparing full-scale production of compact and subcompact cars since the autumn, in an effort to compete with Japanese manufacturers. To protect the American automobile industry, Douglas Fraser, head of the United Automobile Workers, is both pressing the United States government to pass legislation requiring Japanese automakers to build automobile plants within the United States and strongly insisting on Japan's self-restriction of exports. Honda has decided to launch production of cars in the United States, and Datsun will follow with the production of small-sized trucks. Toyota has also been forced to decide to begin manufacturing in the United States in order to avoid being criticized for flooding the market in the United States and Europe. In his New Year's address to his managers, President Toyota called for the "establishment of an epoch-making management system" and the "lowering of costs from the ground up." Rationalization will certainly become more severe.

A certain foreman is said to have grumbled, on his way to the auditorium, "Last year we were pushed to wring water out of a dry towel. What will they tell us to do this year?" The punch line in the address that day was "If there is a steep mountain ahead of us, let us call the mountain to us, level it, and endure difficulties." It seems that Toyota-style rationalization is going to become even more high-handed.

Toyota's production in 1979 reached 2,996,000 units, a 4.9 percent increase over the preceding year. With knockdown sets* included, the number reached 3,070,000—a new record. The ordinary profit for the first half of this year is forecast at $1.1 billion, or an increase of 26 percent over the same period of last year. This, too, is the highest in the company's history. As a result, profit, after taxes, will amount to $590 million. This means that a day's operation will bring to Toyota more than $1.8 million profit.

As of June 1979, the Toyota Motor Company employed 45,233 workers. The increase is only 30 people over the same month last year. On the other hand, the increase in production is marked, an increase of 140,000 vehicles, from 2,930,000 to 3,070,000. Calculated in terms of finished vehicles, this means each worker produces 66 vehicles a year. Ten years ago, the equivalent figure was 49. Even by simple calculation (and taking into account some automation at work), it's clear that labor has been intensified enormously. Furthermore, in those few years Toyota hired few seasonal workers.

It was only twelve years ago that red-and-white sweet rice jelly was handed out to all employees to commemorate the achievement of the production level of 100,000 vehicles per month. Clearly, these recent

---

* Knockdown sets are the vehicles that are sold and exported disassembled to be assembled in another country.

records have been achieved at the expense of the exhaustion of the regular workers. This year the production goal is 3,220,000. The electric lights on the panel will flash on and off still more rapidly.

The keynote of Toyota rationalization is the elimination of all waste:

1. Waste from overproduction
2. Waste in waiting
3. Waste in the shipping process
4. Waste in processing
5. Waste in inventories
6. Waste in motions
7. Waste from producing defective products*

The rationalization here is not so much to eliminate work as, more directly, to eliminate workers. For example, if 33 percent of "wasted motion" is eliminated from three workers, one worker becomes unnecessary. The history of Toyota rationalization is a history of the reduction of workers, and that's the secret of how Toyota shows no increase in employees while achieving its startling increases in production. All free time during working hours has been taken away from assembly-line workers as wasteful. All their time, to the last second, is devoted to production. Subcontractors deliver parts directly to the conveyor belts. Assembly conveyors in each plant are subordinate to the main conveyors that ship out finished cars, and the conveyor belts in subcontracting firms are "synchronized" to the conveyor belts in each Toyota plant. This "kanban method," which has been widely her-

---

* Taiichi Ohno, *The Toyota Method of Production*.

alded in the mass media, is meant to compel subcontractors to deliver parts exactly on time, which is just another sign of the increasing "synchronization" in the industry. Even the streets between the subcontractors and Toyota's plants are regarded as conveyor belts connecting the actual conveyor belts within the plants. The Toyota method of production appears to the outside world as the systematization of "the relationship of a community bound together by a common fate" (Ohno, *Toyota Method of Production*). But truthfully, it's nothing more than the absolute determination to make all movement of goods and people in and out of these plants subordinate to Toyota's will.

It was the silent coercion of the conveyor belt that I felt most strongly while I was working at Toyota. More precisely, it was the merciless directions from the control room at the Head Office. The number and type of vehicles to be produced are probably allocated to each shop through consultation between Toyota and the Toyota Motor Sales Company Ltd. In the transmission assembly shop where I worked, iron flags (a variety of kanban) came down the conveyor belts to designate the type of cars to be produced. These were sent in accordance with the instruction printed out on tapes by the control room. Seeing the color and shape of the flags, workers chose appropriate parts from those on hand. If production was lower because of some minor malfunction of machines, the conveyor speed was increased to make up the delay. If production was delayed owing to a fellow worker's absence, overtime became necessary. Even without such incidents, production goals were always just beyond what seemed like the human capacity to produce, and no worker knew what time he might go home once he was in the shop. The workers were bound to the conveyors until they stopped, and the conveyors never stopped until the production goal for the day was achieved.

Books praise the "kanban method" to the skies, but the real things that make Toyota run haven't changed since I was there in 1973. Basically, Toyota's great leaps in production are achieved through production allowances and a work-quota system. At Toyota, an employee's total monthly wage includes a relatively low basic wage, overtime pay, a production allowance, and various other allowances. The production allowance is that part of an employee's monthly pay which is calculated against the number of work units (that is, the number of worker multiplied by the number of working hours) it takes a team to reach a certain production goal. Basically, wages for the month will increase if the team exceeds the production goal in fewer hours and with less manpower. One worker's monthly wage could fluctuate from month to month by as much as $45, even with the same number of working days and the same amount of overtime. Nobody except the Personnel Department really knows how the wages are computed. In some plants, announcements like the following are made during working hours:

TODAY'S PRODUCTION GOAL IS 565 VEHICLES.
THE LINE HAS STOPPED SIXTY MINUTES.
WORKER TROUBLE RESPONSIBILITY THIRTY MINUTES.

With more hours of "trouble responsibilty," the month's wages would naturally decrease. Should someone in the team make a mistake, the wage would decrease correspondingly. Tied to the conveyor belts, everyone works desperately, hoping that he is not a burden to others. This is the "relationship of a community bound together by a common fate."

A worker says: "I worked four or five hours of overtime last month. This month I worked twelve hours. But the total earnings differ only by $4.50." This is not a rare case at all. The basic wage for a worker who is a high school graduate with eleven years of service is $285 a month. However, the "basic wage-production allowance" as printed on the pay slips fluctuates as follows:

July 1979: $652
October 1979: $647
December 1979: $650

These figures are for a worker off the assembly line, and therefore his productivity can't be measured in the manner outlined above. Nevertheless, his wage fluctuates as shown above.

The pay slips of workers at the conveyor lines—where work quotas are assigned—are not available. But I have heard that their basic pay, including production allowance, would be about twice the basic wage, and that the production allowance would go up and down by a margin of 40 percent. In other words, if a worker's basic wage is $318, his pay will fluctuate between $636 and $763. The quota and production allowance constantly spur workers to increase their output. If the teams put in too much overtime, the production allowance is reduced "because they are inefficient." If the teams should have a successive three-month increase in the production allowance, the number of workers is reduced "because they have too many workers." This is the essence of the Toyota method of production. Introduced around 1960, this is functionally a piecework payment system.

Workers are urged on to production, day and night. So tightly are their lives bound to the conveyor belts in the plants that they cannot even take days off when they want to. The thoroughgoing enforcement of rationalization has eliminated all relief workers. Not only team leaders, the lowest management people, but also unit leaders have been required to work on conveyor lines. Even foremen, normally part of higher management, may sometimes put on working gloves and lend a hand. Then these men have to take home their paperwork such as the writing of daily reports and the calculation of day-by-day work units. Through it all the conveyor belts are kept running, with the absolute minimum number of men necessary.

I can remember times when I was absent from work and someone from the Personnel Department came to the dormitory to get me. One worker, who had to attend to an urgent matter, took a day off only after going to the shop to confirm that all the other workers had arrived. Another worker, who was absent because of illness, was called out to work only to collapse on the line. You could easily find many similar absurd but true stories. The other side of rationalization is compulsory labor.

Workers in Japan are guaranteed annual paid personal holidays (APPH) by the Labor Standards Act. However, 30 percent of Toyota workers were not able to take even a day off in three months. Taking one month, September 1979, as an example, the no-leave rate reached 49 percent for the entire company. The rate was highest at the plants producing the most popular models. Management and union both have encouraged workers to submit requests for leaves once every three months. In other words, by making workers apply for leaves three months in advance, the corporation controls holiday as well as work time. The union's goal is "to make sure that everyone can take planned APPHs once in three months." The company's idea on APPHs, transmitted to workers at before-work meetings, is "APPHs are not a right but a favor given by the company." "Vacation without causing a burden for others" is the slogan repeatedly stressed at Toyota. The number of holidays taken is an important factor in performance appraisals. A sudden absence is called an "unexpected annual leave," and is not only harmful to the worker's future career but may also result in a car from the plant coming to get him within minutes.

In 1979, an issue of the *Toyota Weekly* carried the following part of a question-and-answer article.

Q: It is difficult to take days off since the boss looks displeased and absences will influence my record, won't they?

A: If there are many "unexpected leaves" or if specific people take too many days off, this will mean trouble for your fellow workers, and your boss will indeed be displeased. The mood that you complain of would be dispelled if everyone took leaves in a planned and impartial way. As long as this happens, the management will prove understanding and cooperative.

The root of the workers' difficulty in taking annual paid personal holidays is the extreme reduction of manpower. However, the union's policy is not to demand abolishment of the reward system or the production allowance, which together form the piecework wage system supporting Toyota's incredible increase in productivity. Nor does the union demand more workers. Rather the policy is always "to have talks to promote understanding and cooperation." In 1962 Toyota management and labor issued a "Management-Union Declaration," in which they called for the reduction of costs and the establishment of a mass-production system "in order to overcome this difficult situation with determination." Since then, the labor union has been "resolutely" complying with rationalization. Big headlines—"New Record in Production"— can be found in almost every issue of the *Toyota*, which calls on workers to "challenge the highest peaks with our all-out efforts" (January 1, 1980). For more than ten years management has been spurring workers on at meetings: Don't be caught up by Datsun. Don't drop the market share. Don't be defeated in the small-car war. Don't be a second Chrysler.

In a speech at a management-union convention in early November 1979, President Toyota stressed that "we cannot afford to lose in the competition of the 1980s," and concluded: "The competitors closely following us will make inroads if we lose the spirit of challenge."

The rationalization policy proposed on that day was to make bold and resolute decisions on "strategic investments," such as new plant construction, but to refrain from "investments for the increase of production capacity." This is no more than a fancy way to repeat the Toyota ideology: "With ingenuity and good ideas, we can find a solution to increased orders even beyond our present full capacity, though we know how hard it is." In other words, Toyota will expand its assembly-line facilities, but any increase in production should be managed through the intensification of labor. Speeding up the conveyor belts does not cost money.

When I left Toyota in February 1973, assembly time at the Main Plant for transmissions was one minute and fourteen seconds. This had been shortened by six seconds in the six months since I had begun, while production had been increased by 100 to 415 units. Now, seven years later, the assembly time is forty-five seconds and the production is 690 units. This increase was achieved solely through accelerating the work pace. Knockdown part packing at the Takaoka plant needed sixty minutes for a set (which includes 20 cars) three years ago. Today it takes twelve minutes, and still the manpower has been reduced from 50 to 40. Before, workers stood in front of conveyors; now they rush around from one part to another, pushing mobile work desks with wheels.

At the assembly lines for passenger cars, parts have become larger and have increased in number, owing to exhaust-emission control. In addition, parts for various models come down the line all mixed together because of the simultaneous production of many models. Nevertheless, the speed of the conveyor belts only accelerates. The Tahara plant on the Chita Peninsula, which started its operation in January 1979, recently completed arrangements to produce 5,000 small trucks and 5,000 Corollas. To fill its manpower needs, many workers were taken from the other Toyota plants. Despite this loss, conveyor belts at each plant are running as if nothing had happened. Many workers have been moved onto the assembly line as "reinforcements." Workers are forced to work on Sundays and holidays. The reinforcement work and Sunday-holiday work are a lubricant without which the conveyors could not run.

At the management-union convention mentioned above, Executive Director Yoshiaki Yamamoto said: "In this day and age of uncertainty and severe competition, we must and shall concentrate our production on popular models and adjust the imbalance of work loads among shops. So please be cooperative in establishing flexible shop arrangements that will be able to respond quickly to requests for help."

Reinforcement work is feared by workers who have had no work experience on conveyor lines. Most workers begin losing weight within a few days. Even without the everyday work they're expected to do, inexperienced reinforcement workers would be exhausted by such difficult labor in a totally unfamiliar environment. A directive to management ("On Accepting Reinforcement Workers: Daily Guidance and Management") from the Takaoka plant personnel division shows that reinforcement workers have many complaints and dissatisfactions, more than half of which pertain to safety issues. But the guidance policy goes no farther than the following:

> Management personnel and the long-time workers in the shop should "say hello and a few words" to reinforcement workers at least once a day, and unit members should make an effort to create a congenial atmosphere so that the management and senior workers can easily "say hello and a few words." . . .
> It is not easy for reinforcement workers to speak out.

One evening, I met with workers from various plants. I wanted to know the facts behind Toyota's remarkable production records. What the workers counted on their fingers was the number of suicides—more than twenty in the past year. These were only cases that they remembered at that moment. They told me that in June there were three suicides within a couple of days. There was a twenty-seven-year-old worker at the Takaoka plant who reported to work and then disappeared; he had thrown himself into the sea. A team leader at the same plant drove his car into a reservoir. These were the only cases reported in the newspapers. The other cases were all related by those who had been close to the suicides. There are no statistics.

The number, they said, is particularly high at the Takaoka plant, whose products are popular and whose production cannot keep pace with demand. On June 28, a forty-five-year-old worker at the Tsutsumi plant hanged himself in his company-rented apartment. Around the same time, a Takaoka plant reinforcement worker from the Tsutsumi plant committed suicide in his dormitory by taking sleeping pills. He was depressed after having been blamed by the team leader for his tardiness and forced to "apologize to his fellow workers for the inconvenience he caused." Also around the same time, a team leader of the Maintenance Department in the Head Office hanged himself. A body found at the Takaoka plant dormitory was taken away by a member of the Security Division staff. Afterwards he complained that while playing pinball, he imagined he saw the suicide's face in the glass of the pinball machine. The workers who met with me that evening talked endlessly of similar cases. I had heard rumors of mentally disturbed workers and suicides many times while I worked at Toyota. But the rapid increase in their numbers is frightening.

It is not uncommon these days for big industries to have many injuries and deaths, as well as occupational diseases which are dealt with as away-from-the-job injuries and diseases. However, Toyota's methods of handling these cases are unique, perhaps because of the closed nature of the Toyota community or because the lower management has been so well indoctrinated in the ideology of "Production First." Cases of company-admitted occupational injury and death reached 267 between January and September 1979. Among them, 102 were workers with less than one year's experience, and 71, workers with less than three month's experience (*Safety and Health News*, December 24, 1979). These are the reinforcement workers in unfamiliar surroundings, the newly hired, the newly transferred, trainees, and the like. The work pace has been established, and newcomers who cannot adapt themselves to the speed are repeatedly injured. The foregoing figures bear this out. The acceleration of production also forces the workers to hold their bodies in unnatural postures for long periods of time and has produced many patients with back pains and "shoulder-arm-neck syndrome" (*keikenwan shokogun*). However, the company does not admit these as occupational diseases brought about by the work.

Mr. A entered Toyota as a "mid-career hiree" in September 1974 at thirty-six years of age. He had worked in the kitchen detail of the Maritime Self-Defense Force for five years and then at employee cafeterias and other places. He was assigned to the Takaoka plant, where he put shock absorbers on wheel axles for eight months. There he developed shoulder-arm-neck syndrome. A doctor in the city prescribed three weeks rest and treatment. The plant management forced him to continue working, however, and took him to the doctor by car after work. Finally, he was unable to move; the diagnosis was "acute sinal and nuchal muscle rigidity pain." He asked his boss to assign him lighter work, but the answer was: "There are no light jobs in Toyota. Come back after you have completely recovered, or go somewhere else where they have light work." With the doctor's intercession, he was finally assigned to "Goshiken" and given a job assisting in making fender covers. "Goshiken" was the workshop for the sickly and suffering workers. Officially it did not exist; when company executives made their visits, the workers had to hide themselves. There were no year-end or New Year parties in this workshop. No company newsletters were circulated. It was an island for exiles. Later, Mr. A was transferred to work installing air conditioners, and then to a fitting-out line. He now complains of "lower-back contusion," "hernia of the intervertebral disk," and "muscle-strain aggravation symptoms."

In October 1979, he was notified by the Head Office's Personnel Department that he would be discharged in a month owing to the expiration of his leave-of-absence period. (The discharge of occupational-disease patients is prohibited by law.) But whether out of ignorance of or indifference to the law, the company stated that it "hasn't admitted Mr. A.'s disease as an occupational disease even if the Labor Standards Inspection Office has." There have been plenty of similar episodes at Toyota. While warning against the rising number of accidents, a team leader is said to have told workers at a meeting in the Main Plant, "Your injuries won't trouble the company much. Only your family will be in difficulty." The labor union won't touch the work-injury and occupational-disease issue. Gradually management has become more and more high-handed without being checked by the union. Thus, normal sensitivity becomes dulled at the workshops.

As regards Mr. A, the Takaoka plant personnel division eventually withdrew the discharge notice after receiving a decision from the Inspection Office to start the payment of Workmen's Compensation benefits. And this came only under pressure from a small workers' group and the Toyota District Labor Council.

While management journalism may applaud Toyota's high profit and the "kanban method" which they see as supporting it, the human costs of Toyota methods—suicides, injuries, job fatalities, and occupational disease—increase at a horrifying rate. The situation at Toyota is a sad but typical example of the victimization of workers in modern society. Workers suffer every day in front of conveyor belts. The panel in Toyota Hall increases every six seconds. Whenever I come to this city and talk with the workers, I feel as though I have strayed into some fantasy land. But this is a nightmare that I have lived, and the anger will not go away.

About the Author

SATOSHI KAMATA, the author of numerous books, is one of Japan's leading free-lance journalists. A graduate of Waseda University in 1964, he was employed for a time by a trade paper in the steel industry and as an editor for a popular general magazine. Since 1965 he has worked as a full-time free-lance reporter, and his work has appeared in major newspapers and magazines throughout Japan. This is his first book to be published in the United States.

About the Translator/Editor

TATSURU AKIMOTO, a graduate of Tokyo Metropolitan University with a degree in labor law, has himself written numerous articles in Japan on the problems of the automobile industry and labor in general. He was previously a lecturer at the Japan School of Social Work. His researches have brought him to the United States a number of times, most recently on a Fulbright grant.

Professor Ronald Dore has asked that this statement of his be included in each copy of Japan in the Passing Lane, *because of his concern that protectionists in the United States may misuse what Satoshi Kamata has to say.*

Although written in 1972, this is a highly topical book. The world is in its worst slump for fifty years and protectionist urges in the richest countries threaten to make it worse. All over America and Europe are people who will seize on Mr. Kamata's story to say:

> Here at last is the secret of Japan's competitiveness. Here is proof of the social dumping we have always alleged.

They would, in my view, be wrong. To say that Mr. Kamata's story tells us *the* secret of the Japanese miracle is as misleading as it would be to say that the pay and conditions in some of the textile factories in the U.S. South are *the* reasons why American exports wiped out whole sections of the British household textiles industry in 1980.

We at Pantheon Books share this view and would like to make clear that nothing said in our jacket description should be construed in a contrary sense.